Chicago Top 40 Charts
1980–1990

Chicago Top 40 Charts 1980–1990

Compiled by Ron Smith

Writers Club Press
San Jose New York Lincoln Shanghai

Chicago Top 40 Charts 1980–1990

Writers Club Press
an imprint of iUniverse, Inc.

For information address:
iUniverse, Inc.
5220 S. 16th St., Suite 200
Lincoln, NE 68512
www.iuniverse.com

ISBN: 0-595-22626-4

Printed in the United States of America

To the memory of Art Roberts—an example, a mentor and a very good friend. Excelsior, Art!

CONTENTS

ACKNOWLEDGEMENTS

Thank you to those who inspired, encouraged and helped as I compiled and promoted these books: Chuck Bern, Clark Besch, Dick Biondi, John Charleson, Steve Dahl, Dave Douglas, Dennis Dvorshak, J.R. Dykema, Tommy Edwards, Mike Elder, Robert Feder, Scott Fischer, Jim Furholmen, Bill Ganson, John Gehron, John Govi, Barbara Jastrab, Randy Lane, Donald Liebenson, Dan Lusk, Jack Miller, Mark Morris, Dale Noble, Lorna Ozmon, Scott Paulson, Robert Pruter, Jeff Roteman, Randy Rowley, Kurt Scholle, Hank Shurba, Dan Silvia, Bob Sirott, Jim Smith, Bill Stedman and Clark Weber. A big "thank you" goes to Scott Childers, without whom this edition would probably not have been possible. As always, a special thanks goes to the person who inspires every book of this type, Joel Whitburn.

INTRODUCTION

Welcome as we conclude our journey through the Windy City's most popular music as determined by the weekly music surveys issued by radio stations WLS and its FM counterpart, WYTZ.

Transition and change. Those were the watchwords for the ABC-owned radio stations in Chicago in the 1980s.

WLS-AM was still a dominant force in the market as the decade opened, having weathered the storm of disco music much better than its FM sister, then known as "Disco DAI". WDAI soon switched to contemporary music itself as WRCK before simulcasting mornings and evenings as WLS-FM.

The handwriting was on the wall for AM top 40, though, as FM listening was finally surpassing AM, even in Chicago. Rather than wait and become a victim of the trend away from music on that band, WLS-AM began a slow transition towards talk radio.

WLS disk jockeys were encouraged to talk more and full-fledged sex and sports talk shows arrived on the station. By mid-1981, the printed chart started promoting both WLS-AM and FM. Four years later, the AM station was unceremoniously dropped from the survey. By this time, WLS-AM's music (when there was music) was a blend of contemporary hits, oldies and even adult standards. By 1989, with their ratings at the lowest level ever, it wasn't a question of whether to stop playing music altogether, but when. On August 23 of that year, the last song was played on WLS-AM ("Just You 'N' Me" by Chicago) and the station was shortly reborn as "Talkradio 89". Today, WLS-AM is one of the dominant stations in the Windy City and still fiercely proud of its musical heritage.

The printed survey had continued on without interruption, now clearly promoting WLS-FM. By January of 1986, the call letters were changed to WYTZ (Z95) to distance the FM from the faltering AM. And the survey underwent a name change as well in November of that year, becoming the "Z95 Street Sheet".

The charts generally listed 45 songs with as many as 19 "extras" for most of the decade. Clearly the conservative playlists of the mid-1970s were gone as on August 9, 1986, 59 songs appeared on the survey!

The station also supported local acts with a ferocity not seen since the mid-1960s. Besides the expected Styx, Survivor and Chicago tunes, the station pushed such Chicago-based groups as Off Broadway, Ministry and Flesh For Lulu.

WYTZ found itself locked into a battle with WBBM-FM (B96) for the top 40 crown that was, in its way, even more fierce than the WLS/WCFL "radio wars" two decades earlier. But this time, the ABC station found itself on the losing end of the battle. Mirroring its successful tactics from the 1970s, the station's playlist began to shrink. The printed survey only listed 40 tunes by January of 1987. By years-end, the list was down to 30. In September of 1989, only 25 songs appeared, though seven weeks later it expanded to 30 songs again and continued that size for the remainder of its existence.

WYTZ went so far in its fight for ratings as to bring in consultant Randy Michaels (now programming head of Clear Channel Communications, owners of contemporary WKSC-FM in Chicago), who tried to draw attention to the station by (among other gimmicks) renaming it "Hell". The stunt backfired and the station's ratings, already less-than-stellar, went to its namesake. It quickly retreated to the more modest "Hot 94.7".

Hot 94.7 was a more mainstream station than B96 and it showed in the number of heavy metal and alternative tunes that appeared on its chart. The station was also not afraid to play album cuts by established artists and bring back older tunes used at the time in current movies.

The rise of cassettes and CDs as singles became less important and the loss of "mom and pop" record stores in favor of giant chains that didn't rely on station surveys to stock music from are probably responsible for the demise of the printed survey. In any event, the last printed WYTZ Street Sheet appeared for the week of May 5, 1990—thirty years to the day (May 2) that WLS-AM first started playing top 40 music. While the station sent a copy of their playlist to record stores for the next five months, distribution of those reports became spotty until they ceased as well. WYTZ itself would last less than two more years before again becoming WLS-FM and simulcasting the talk shows of its AM sister station. After failed attempts at "hip talk", country and 1980s music, the station (now called WZZN, "The Zone") currently airs alternative music.

Over their nearly 30-year span, over 1,500 surveys were issued by WLS and WYTZ. It's been my pleasure in the three volumes in this series to record that information for posterity and to re-introduce Chicago to its musical heritage.

METHODOLOGY

This book is a continuation of *Chicago Top 40 Charts 1960-1969* and *Chicago Top 40 Charts 1970-1979* and covers every tune that charted on the WLS-AM, WLS-FM and WYTZ-FM weekly music surveys from January 5, 1980 through the final printed survey on May 5, 1990.

As in the previous books, **Debut** is the date the song first appears on the charts. **Peak** is the date it first reaches its highest position. **Pos** is the highest position reached on the charts and **Wks** is the number of weeks it appears on the charts.

In most years, special year-end charts took the place of the normal survey. As before, songs that appeared on the charts before and after the special survey are given credit for the missing week. Songs debuting after the special survey are not credited for the previous week, even when their debut position is rather high. Songs that drop off the chart after a special survey are not credited for the missing week. During any missing weeks, all songs not appearing are considered "frozen" at their previous position but are given credit for the week on the chart.

At times, "two-sided hits" appeared on the charts. Both the "A" and "B" sides of a record would be listed. Any time both sides were listed, the "B" side also received credit for the position reached and that week on the chart. However, often the "B" side was only listed during part of the record's run on the chart. Only the weeks a "B" side was actually listed is credited. So "Ballerina Girl" by Lionel Richie is given credit for reaching #3 on the chart, the same as its flip side, "Deep River Woman". But it receives credit for five less weeks because only "Deep River Woman" was listed for the first month. In the artist listing, "B" sides are preceded by a slash and listed under their "A" sides.

1

Artists often recorded under different variations of their names. Name variations are indented under the original artist name. Totally different groups or names are listed separately, with a notation to "also see" the other artist.

The size of the WLS/WYTZ charts was generally 45 songs with as many as 14 "extra" tunes (late in the decade, the number of tunes shrunk to 30 and even 25 but extras still appeared). Since the extra songs were in rank order, credit was given to them as if numbering continued. So the three extra songs listed on the January 26, 1980 survey were credited here as #46 through #48.

The yearly top 40 lists are not the printed WLS year-end lists, but rather my own objective ranking of the year's (and decade's) top songs, based on highest position reached, weeks at that highest position, weeks on the chart, followed by weeks in the top ten, twenty and top five, in that order.

In the past, charted songs have come back to appear again after several years ("Wipe Out" by the Surfaris comes to mind). My policy has always been to treat this event as a separate chart entry. That practice continues in this book. On a few occasions during the 1980s, a song charted for a week or two as an album cut, then returned months later as a single. Using my established practice, the song is listed twice. One particularly vexing test of this policy, though, occurred with the song "Chains Of Love" by Erasure. The song made a modest 5-week run up the chart, peaking at #19. Then after being off the chart for six weeks, it reappeared and made a second 3-week run to #16. While it is odd to see a song listed twice in two months, I felt it was ultimately less confusing to separate the appearances. Those who disagree are free to combine them together.

Finally, the top artists of the decade is based on a point system for the highest position reached for every charted song by an artist with bonus points for each week on the chart.

ALPHABETICAL LISTING BY ARTIST

Artist	Title	Debut	Peak	Pos	Wks
ABBA					
	The Winner Takes It All	2/14/81	3/21/81	12	14
	When All Is Said And Done	1/30/82	3/13/82	16	11
also see Frida					
Abbott, Gregory					
	Shake You Down	11/29/86	1/24/87	4	13
ABC					
	The Look Of Love (Part One)	11/13/82	12/18/82	10	19
	Poison Arrow	3/19/83	4/16/83	22	11
	Be Near Me	9/28/85	11/16/85	17	12
	(How To Be A) Millionaire	3/8/86	3/22/86	33	5
	When Smokey Sings	7/4/87	8/29/87	19	11
Abdul, Paula					
	Straight Up	1/14/89	2/25/89	1	17
	Forever Your Girl	4/1/89	5/13/89	4	15
	Cold Hearted	7/15/89	8/26/89	3	16
	(It's Just) The Way That You Love Me	9/23/89	11/18/89	4	16
Abdul, Paula with the Wild Pair					
	Opposites Attract	1/13/90	2/17/90	1	17
AC/DC					
	You Shook Me All Night Long	11/15/80	1/10/81	15	26
	Back In Black	2/14/81	3/21/81	11	17
	Let's Get It Up	1/16/82	2/20/82	16	11
Adams, Bryan					
	Lonely Nights	2/20/82	4/3/82	33	15
	Straight From The Heart	4/23/83	5/14/83	13	16
	Cuts Like A Knife	6/25/83	7/23/83	22	11
	This Time	10/15/83	11/12/83	30	7
	Heaven	4/14/84	4/21/84	46	2
	Run To You	12/8/84	1/26/85	9	14
	Somebody	3/9/85	4/6/85	18	11
	Heaven	4/20/85	6/22/85	4	19

Artist	Title	Debut	Peak	Pos	Wks
	Summer Of '69	6/29/85	8/17/85	9	16
	One Night Love Affair	9/14/85	11/9/85	23	12
	Heat Of The Night	4/18/87	5/23/87	15	7
Adams, Bryan & Tina Turner					
	It's Only Love	12/21/85	1/25/86	28	8
also see Turner, Tina					
Aerosmith					
	Dude (Looks Like A Lady)	11/7/87	12/19/87	13	11
	Angel	3/26/88	4/23/88	7	12
	Rag Doll	6/25/88	7/30/88	7	10
	Love In An Elevator	9/16/89	10/21/89	11	7
	Janie's Got A Gun	1/20/90	2/24/90	2	13
	What It Takes	4/21/90	5/5/90	25	3
After The Fire					
	Der Kommissar	3/5/83	5/7/83	8	20
a-ha					
	Take On Me	7/27/85	9/21/85	5	22
	The Sun Always Shines On T.V.	12/28/85	2/15/86	24	12
	Cry Wolf	2/7/87	3/21/87	22	7
Air Supply					
	Lost In Love	4/5/80	6/7/80	1	34
	All Out Of Love	8/16/80	10/4/80	3	27
	Every Woman In The World	11/29/80	1/31/81	10	18
	The One That You Love	6/20/81	8/1/81	6	21
	Here I Am (Just When I Thought I Was Over You)	11/7/81	12/19/81	7	15
	Sweet Dreams	2/6/82	4/17/82	17	17
	Even The Nights Are Better	7/31/82	8/21/82	10	14
	Making Love Out Of Nothing At All	9/17/83	10/22/83	2	20
	Just As I Am	7/20/85	8/3/85	32	7
Al B. Sure!					
	Nite And Day	6/4/88	7/2/88	7	8
Allen, Donna					
	Serious	4/11/87	5/9/87	20	6

Artist Title	Debut	Peak	Pos	Wks
Alpert, Herb				
Rise	9/8/79	10/27/79	1	23
Diamonds	5/2/87	6/20/87	6	13
Alphaville				
Forever Young	11/19/88	12/10/88	17	4
Ambrosia				
Biggest Part Of Me	5/3/80	6/21/80	9	20
You're The Only Woman (You & I)	9/6/80	10/11/80	23	10
America				
You Can Do Magic	9/11/82	10/30/82	6	19
Anderson, John				
Swingin'	4/16/83	5/14/83	12	14
Animotion				
Obsession	3/23/85	4/27/85	7	16
Ant, Adam				
Goody Two Shoes	12/25/82	2/19/83	5	18
April Wine				
Just Between You And Me	3/7/81	4/18/81	9	19
Arcadia				
Election Day	10/26/85	12/21/85	6	16
also see Duran Duran				
Archangel, Natalie				
Mr. Perfect For Me	7/25/87	8/8/87	39	3
Art Of Noise with Max Headroom				
Paranoimia	8/23/86	10/4/86	29	9
Art Of Noise featuring Tom Jones				
Kiss	11/26/88	12/24/88	15	5
Ashford & Simpson				
Solid	2/9/85	3/23/85	12	12
Asia				
Heat Of The Moment	5/1/82	6/19/82	6	24
Only Time Will Tell	8/7/82	9/18/82	9	14

Artist	Title	Debut	Peak	Pos	Wks
	Don't Cry	7/30/83	9/17/83	8	15

also see GTR and Yes

Astley, Rick

	Title	Debut	Peak	Pos	Wks
	Never Gonna Give You Up	2/6/88	3/26/88	1	17
	Together Forever	5/7/88	6/25/88	3	13
	It Would Take A Strong Strong Man	9/3/88	9/24/88	11	6
	She Wants To Dance With Me	12/10/88	2/4/89	2	14

Atlantic Starr

	Title	Debut	Peak	Pos	Wks
	Secret Lovers	2/15/86	4/5/86	3	15
	Always	4/18/87	6/6/87	1	15

also see Bryant, Sharon

Austin, Patti with James Ingram

	Title	Debut	Peak	Pos	Wks
	Baby, Come To Me	12/25/82	1/29/83	1	20

also see Ingram, James with Michael McDonald

Babyface

	Title	Debut	Peak	Pos	Wks
	Whip Appeal	4/21/90	5/5/90	18	3

also see the Deele

Bad English

	Title	Debut	Peak	Pos	Wks
	When I See You Smile	10/7/89	11/18/89	1	19
	Price Of Love	3/17/90	4/7/90	15	5

also see Journey and Waite, John

Bailey, Philip with Phil Collins

	Title	Debut	Peak	Pos	Wks
	Easy Lover	12/22/84	2/2/85	1	18

also see Collins, Phil and Earth, Wind & Fire

Baker, Anita

	Title	Debut	Peak	Pos	Wks
	Sweet Love	9/27/86	11/1/86	16	13
	Same Ole Love (365 Days A Year)	5/2/87	6/6/87	21	7
	Giving You The Best That I Got	11/12/88	12/17/88	5	10
	Just Because	3/25/89	4/8/89	22	4

Balin, Marty

	Title	Debut	Peak	Pos	Wks
	Hearts	7/25/81	8/22/81	20	12

also see Jefferson Starship and the KBC Band

Baltimora

	Title	Debut	Peak	Pos	Wks
	Tarzan Boy	1/25/86	3/8/86	7	13

Artist	Title	Debut	Peak	Pos	Wks
Bananarama					
	Cruel Summer	9/8/84	10/6/84	7	12
	Venus	7/5/86	9/6/86	1	19
	I Heard A Rumour	9/5/87	10/10/87	7	13
Band Aid					
	Do They Know It's Christmas	1/5/85	1/12/85	1	9
also see Geldof, Bob					
Bangles					
	Manic Monday	3/1/86	4/19/86	8	15
	If She Knew What She Wants	6/14/86	7/5/86	30	7
	Walk Like An Egyptian	11/1/86	12/13/86	1	18
	Walking Down Your Street	3/14/87	4/25/87	15	8
	Hazy Shade Of Winter	11/28/87	1/30/88	2	16
	In Your Room	11/5/88	1/7/89	5	11
	Eternal Flame	2/4/89	4/8/89	1	16
Basil, Toni					
	Mickey	11/20/82	12/11/82	1	23
Beach Boys					
	The Beach Boys Medley	8/29/81	9/26/81	16	12
	Come Go With Me	1/23/82	2/13/82	31	6
	Getcha Back	6/22/85	7/13/85	32	8
	California Dreamin'	10/18/86	11/22/86	44	8
	Kokomo	10/1/88	11/5/88	1	16
also see the Fat Boys & the Beach Boys					
Beastie Boys					
	(You Gotta) Fight For Your Right (To Party)	1/24/87	3/7/87	2	11
	Brass Monkey	3/21/87	5/2/87	21	8
	Hey Ladies	8/5/89	8/26/89	12	7
Beatles					
	The Beatles' Movie Medley	4/17/82	5/15/82	13	11
also see Lennon, John; Harrison, George and McCartney, Paul					
Belew, Adrian					
	Oh Daddy	7/29/89	8/26/89	10	8

Artist	Title	Debut	Peak	Pos	Wks
Bell Biv DeVoe					
	Poison	4/21/90	5/5/90	16	3
also see New Edition					
Belle Stars					
	Iko Iko	1/28/89	3/4/89	7	9
Benatar, Pat					
	Heartbreaker	3/8/80	4/12/80	6	20
	Hit Me With Your Best Shot	11/8/80	1/17/81	2	29
	Treat Me Right	1/17/81	3/7/81	10	15
	Fire And Ice	7/18/81	8/22/81	10	19
	Shadows Of The Night	10/23/82	11/27/82	7	20
	Love Is A Battlefield	10/22/83	12/3/83	8	17
	We Belong	10/27/84	12/22/84	9	18
	Invincible (Theme From The Legend Of Billie Jean)	6/22/85	8/10/85	23	15
	Sometimes The Good Guys Finish First	8/1/87	8/15/87	40	3
	All Fired Up	7/16/88	8/13/88	20	5
Benson, George					
	Give Me The Night	9/6/80	9/20/80	17	13
	Turn Your Love Around	1/16/82	2/13/82	11	14
Berlin					
	No More Words	5/19/84	6/9/84	21	11
	Take My Breath Away	7/19/86	9/27/86	8	17
	Like Flames	11/8/86	11/15/86	49	2
B-52's					
	Rock Lobster	5/24/80	6/14/80	20	12
	Love Shack	8/26/89	11/11/89	5	25
	Roam	1/13/90	3/10/90	4	17
Bianco, Matt					
	Wap Bam Boogie	11/19/88	12/31/88	8	9
Big Country					
	In A Big Country	11/19/83	12/17/83	13	14
Big Pig					
	Breakaway	3/12/88	4/30/88	15	9

Artist	Title	Debut	Peak	Pos	Wks
Blondie					
	Dreaming	11/24/79	12/15/79	23	12
	Call Me	3/8/80	4/12/80	1	27
	The Tide Is High	12/13/80	2/14/81	3	24
	Rapture	2/21/81	4/25/81	2	17
	also see Harry, Debbie				
Blow Monkeys					
	Digging Your Scene	6/7/86	7/5/86	26	10
Blue Oyster Cult					
	Burnin' For You	8/8/81	10/24/81	15	19
Blue Zone U.K.					
	Jackie	8/6/88	8/20/88	28	3
	also see Stansfield, Lisa				
Blues Brothers					
	Gimme Some Lovin'	6/28/80	8/9/80	3	18
Bolton, Michael					
	(Sittin' On) The Dock Of The Bay	3/12/88	3/12/88	25	2
	How Am I Supposed To Live Without You	12/30/89	2/3/90	1	18
	How Can We Be Lovers	4/7/90	5/5/90	4	5
Bon Jovi					
	You Give Love A Bad Name	10/11/86	11/29/86	1	16
	Livin' On A Prayer	12/13/86	2/21/87	1	18
	Wanted Dead Or Alive	4/11/87	5/30/87	10	11
	Edge Of A Broken Heart	8/22/87	10/3/87	10	12
	Bad Medicine	9/24/88	10/29/88	3	10
	Born To Be My Baby	12/3/88	1/21/89	4	14
	I'll Be There For You	3/11/89	5/6/89	4	11
	Lay Your Hands On Me	6/10/89	8/12/89	4	12
	Living In Sin	11/4/89	11/25/89	17	10
Bonds, Gary U.S.					
	This Little Girl	5/16/81	6/27/81	17	14
	Out Of Work	7/24/82	9/4/82	11	13
Bonoff, Karla					
	Personally	7/10/82	7/31/82	19	13

Artist Title	Debut	Peak	Pos	Wks
Boris Badenough				
Hey Rocky	1/17/87	1/31/87	35	3
Boston				
Amanda	10/4/86	11/8/86	1	16
We're Ready	12/13/86	2/14/87	16	11
Can'tcha Say (You Believe In Me)/Still In Love	2/21/87	4/18/87	14	11
Bowie, David				
Let's Dance	4/9/83	5/14/83	2	25
Blue Jean	9/22/84	11/3/84	7	14
Absolute Beginners	4/12/86	5/10/86	29	8
Day-In Day-Out	5/2/87	5/23/87	24	5
Bowie, David & the Pat Metheny Group				
This Is Not America	3/2/85	3/23/85	22	8
also see Jagger, Mick & David Bowie				
Boys				
Dial My Heart	1/21/89	2/11/89	13	6
Boys Club				
I Remember Holding You	12/10/88	1/28/89	11	8
also see the Jets				
Boys Don't Cry				
I Wanna Be A Cowboy	5/24/86	6/21/86	4	11
Branigan, Laura				
Gloria	10/30/82	11/27/82	1	27
Solitaire	4/30/83	6/4/83	15	13
How Am I Supposed To Live Without You	9/17/83	10/22/83	15	13
Self Control	6/2/84	7/14/84	4	16
The Lucky One	9/8/84	9/29/84	28	9
Moonlight On Water	3/24/90	4/7/90	26	4
Breakfast Club				
Right On Track	3/21/87	5/2/87	10	9
Breathe				
Hands To Heaven	7/9/88	8/20/88	1	11
How Can I Fall	10/8/88	11/12/88	13	10
Don't Tell Me Lies	3/4/89	3/25/89	18	4

Artist Title	Debut	Peak	Pos	Wks
Brickell, Edie & New Bohemians				
What I Am	1/21/89	2/25/89	2	9
Briley, Martin				
The Salt In My Tears	7/30/83	9/10/83	20	13
Brothers Johnson				
Stomp	4/19/80	6/7/80	20	13
Brown, Bobby				
Don't Be Cruel	9/10/88	10/29/88	13	8
My Prerogative	10/15/88	12/3/88	7	14
Roni	2/4/89	3/18/89	10	10
Every Little Step	4/22/89	5/20/89	9	9
On Our Own	7/29/89	9/2/89	5	9
Rock Wit'cha	10/21/89	11/11/89	11	7
also see New Edition				
Brown, James				
Living In America	12/21/85	2/15/86	7	18
Brown, Miquel				
So Many Men - So Little Time	11/12/83	1/14/84	18	21
Browne, Jackson				
Boulevard	8/9/80	9/6/80	10	15
That Girl Could Sing	10/11/80	11/15/80	20	12
Somebody's Baby	8/28/82	10/2/82	6	16
Lawyers In Love	8/6/83	9/17/83	12	14
Tender Is The Night	11/19/83	12/10/83	27	10
For America	3/29/86	4/26/86	27	7
In The Shape Of A Heart	5/24/86	6/28/86	42	7
also see Clemons, Clarence & Jackson Browne				
Bryant, Sharon				
Foolish Heart	12/16/89	12/16/89	29	1
also see Atlantic Starr				
Bryson, Peabo & Roberta Flack				
Tonight, I Celebrate My Love	11/5/83	12/3/83	10	16
Bryson, Peabo				
If Ever You're In My Arms Again	7/28/84	9/8/84	9	14
also see Flack, Roberta				

Artist Title	Debut	Peak	Pos	Wks
Buckingham, Lindsey				
Trouble	12/12/81	2/6/82	13	15
Go Insane	9/8/84	10/13/84	18	11
also see Fleetwood Mac				
Buckner & Garcia				
Pac-Man Fever	2/13/82	4/10/82	3	19
Burnette, Rocky				
Tired Of Toein' The Line	6/14/80	8/2/80	7	18
Cafferty, John & the Beaver Brown Band				
On The Dark Side	9/22/84	11/10/84	15	16
Tender Years	1/19/85	2/2/85	40	5
Tough All Over	5/18/85	6/22/85	33	9
C-I-T-Y	8/31/85	9/21/85	35	7
Pride & Passion	7/22/89	7/29/89	27	2
Calloway				
I Wanna Be Rich	4/14/90	5/5/90	7	4
Cameo				
Word Up	10/4/86	11/15/86	3	17
Back And Forth	5/9/87	5/23/87	32	4
Capaldi, Jim				
Living On The Edge	8/13/83	9/10/83	31	13
Captain & Tennille				
Do That To Me One More Time	12/8/79	2/16/80	5	21
Cara, Irene				
Fame	8/30/80	9/27/80	18	14
Flashdance... What A Feeling	5/7/83	5/28/83	1	29
Why Me	12/10/83	1/14/84	22	13
Breakdance	5/19/84	6/16/84	10	13
Carey, Tony				
A Fine Fine Day	5/5/84	5/26/84	28	8
Carlisle, Belinda				
Mad About You	7/5/86	8/16/86	4	14
Heaven Is a Place On Earth	9/26/87	11/28/87	1	22
I Get Weak	2/6/88	3/19/88	5	12

Artist	Title	Debut	Peak	Pos	Wks
	Circle In The Sand	4/30/88	6/18/88	6	10
	Leave A Light On	10/14/89	11/18/89	10	12

also see the Go-Go's

Carmen, Eric
	Hungry Eyes	1/9/88	2/20/88	2	14
	Make Me Lose Control	7/30/88	9/3/88	5	8

Carnes, Kim
	More Love	7/19/80	9/6/80	14	15
	Bette Davis Eyes	5/2/81	5/30/81	1	22
	Draw Of The Cards	9/5/81	9/26/81	23	9

also see Rogers, Kenny with Kim Carnes

Carrack, Paul
	Don't Shed A Tear	1/23/88	2/20/88	8	6
	I Live By The Groove	11/18/89	12/9/89	17	5

also see Mike + the Mechanics; Lowe, Nick; Roxy Music and Squeeze

Cars
	Shake It Up	12/19/81	2/13/82	6	20
	Since You're Gone	4/17/82	5/15/82	21	10
	You Might Think	3/24/84	5/5/84	8	18
	Magic	6/16/84	7/28/84	18	13
	Drive	8/4/84	9/1/84	12	18
	Hello Again	11/24/84	12/15/84	29	9
	Tonight She Comes	11/2/85	12/21/85	10	16
	I'm Not The One	3/1/86	3/29/86	43	5

also see Ocasek, Ric and Orr, Benjamin

Cetera, Peter
	Livin' In The Limelight	2/6/82	3/6/82	29	9
	Glory Of Love	6/7/86	8/2/86	2	20
	One Good Woman	8/20/88	9/24/88	9	7

Cetera, Peter with Amy Grant
	The Next Time I Fall	9/20/86	12/6/86	6	17

also see Chicago

Chapman, Tracy
	Fast Car	8/20/88	9/10/88	2	6

Artist Title	Debut	Peak	Pos	Wks
Charlene				
I've Never Been To Me	5/8/82	6/5/82	6	14
Charlie				
It's Inevitable	7/30/83	8/20/83	34	8
Cheap Trick				
Dream Police	10/13/79	12/8/79	8	19
Voices	1/26/80	2/23/80	28	9
Stop This Game	11/29/80	2/14/81	27	15
If You Want My Love	6/5/82	7/31/82	23	15
Tonight It's You	7/27/85	10/5/85	24	15
The Flame	6/18/88	7/23/88	1	13
Don't Be Cruel	9/10/88	10/22/88	5	8
also see Wilson, Ann & Robin Zander				
Cher				
If I Could Turn Back Time	9/9/89	10/14/89	1	11
Cherry, Neneh				
Buffalo Stance	5/6/89	6/17/89	1	16
Chicago				
Hard To Say I'm Sorry/Getaway	6/12/82	8/21/82	1	28
Love Me Tomorrow	10/9/82	11/13/82	15	16
Stay The Night	6/2/84	6/30/84	16	14
Hard Habit To Break	8/25/84	10/20/84	6	21
You're The Inspiration	11/24/84	2/2/85	6	18
Along Comes A Woman	2/23/85	4/13/85	26	12
25 Or 6 To 4	10/4/86	10/25/86	43	4
Will You Still Love Me	12/20/86	2/21/87	7	12
If She Would Have Been Faithful	5/2/87	5/23/87	35	4
I Don't Wanna Live Without Your Love	7/2/88	8/27/88	5	11
Look Away	10/8/88	12/10/88	2	13
You're Not Alone	2/18/89	3/18/89	20	6
What Kind Of Man Would I Be	1/6/90	2/10/90	15	10
also see Cetera, Peter				
Chicago Bears Shufflin' Crew				
Superbowl Shuffle	12/21/85	1/11/86	1	14

Artist	Title	Debut	Peak	Pos	Wks
Christopher, Gavin					
	One Step Closer To You	7/19/86	8/23/86	31	9
Cinderella					
	Nobody's Fool	1/24/87	2/21/87	13	6
	Don't Know What You Got (Till It's Gone)	10/8/88	11/19/88	6	9
	The Last Mile	2/25/89	3/18/89	27	4
Clapton, Eric					
	I Can't Stand It	3/28/81	5/2/81	15	13
	I've Got A Rock N' Roll Heart	3/12/83	4/2/83	15	14
	Forever Man	4/20/85	5/4/85	25	7
Clash					
	Train In Vain (Stand By Me)	5/3/80	6/14/80	15	16
	Rock The Casbah	12/11/82	1/22/83	6	18
Clemons, Clarence & Jackson Browne					
	You're A Friend Of Mine	11/16/85	1/25/86	11	16
also see Browne, Jackson and Springsteen, Bruce					
Climax Blues Band					
	I Love You	5/23/81	7/4/81	3	18
Climie Fisher					
	Love Changes (Everything)	8/6/88	8/13/88	25	2
also see Naked Eyes					
Club Nouveau					
	Lean On Me	1/24/87	3/21/87	1	18
	Why You Treat Me So Bad	7/4/87	7/25/87	27	5
Cock Robin					
	When Your Heart Is Weak	8/10/85	9/21/85	41	9
Cocker, Joe & Jennifer Warnes					
	Up Where We Belong	9/18/82	10/16/82	1	20
Cocker, Joe					
	When The Night Comes	12/2/89	1/20/90	4	9
also see Medley, Bill & Jennifer Warnes					
Cole, Natalie					
	Jump Start	9/12/87	10/17/87	11	7
	I Live For Your Love	12/12/87	2/6/88	7	10

Artist	Title	Debut	Peak	Pos	Wks
	Pink Cadillac	3/5/88	4/30/88	1	18
	Miss You Like Crazy	7/8/89	7/29/89	14	5

Collins, Phil
	I Missed Again	4/25/81	5/16/81	10	15
	In The Air Tonight	5/30/81	7/4/81	4	17
	You Can't Hurry Love	12/11/82	1/8/83	12	16
	I Don't Care Anymore	2/12/83	3/19/83	24	12
	Against All Odds (Take A Look At Me Now)	3/10/84	4/7/84	2	21
	One More Night	2/9/85	3/30/85	3	18
	Sussudio	5/11/85	7/20/85	2	17
	Don't Lose My Number	7/6/85	9/7/85	9	18
	Take Me Home	3/22/86	4/26/86	10	15
	We Said Hello, Goodbye	1/2/88	1/30/88	22	6
	Groovy Kind Of Love	9/17/88	10/29/88	1	13
	Two Hearts	12/3/88	1/14/89	2	12
	Another Day In Paradise	11/11/89	12/16/89	2	16
	I Wish It Would Rain Down	2/3/90	3/17/90	5	14

Collins, Phil & Marilyn Martin
	Separate Lives	10/5/85	11/30/85	1	23

also see Bailey, Philip with Phil Collins; Genesis and Martin, Marilyn

Commodores
	Sail On	9/15/79	11/3/79	5	20
	Still	11/3/79	12/15/79	5	19
	Oh No	12/19/81	1/9/82	21	10
	Nightshift	3/30/85	4/27/85	6	14
	Animal Instinct	6/29/85	7/27/85	45	5

also see Richie, Lionel

Communards
	Don't Leave Me This Way	1/17/87	3/7/87	15	9

Company B
	Fascinated	5/2/87	6/13/87	5	12

Contours
	Do You Love Me	6/11/88	7/9/88	14	6

Cooper, Alice
	Poison	10/28/89	11/25/89	7	11

Artist	Title	Debut	Peak	Pos	Wks
Cougar, John					
	Hurts So Good	5/29/82	7/24/82	2	25
	Jack & Diane	7/31/82	9/25/82	1	21
	Hand To Hold On To	12/11/82	1/22/83	24	11
John Cougar Mellencamp					
	Crumblin' Down	11/12/83	12/10/83	17	12
	Pink Houses	1/7/84	2/18/84	17	13
	Authority Song	4/14/84	5/12/84	17	12
	Lonely Ol' Night	8/17/85	10/12/85	9	17
	Small Town	11/2/85	12/21/85	11	17
	R.O.C.K. In The U.S.A.	2/1/86	3/29/86	5	16
	Rain On The Scarecrow	5/17/86	6/7/86	21	7
	Rumbleseat	6/28/86	8/16/86	25	11
	Paper In Fire	10/3/87	10/17/87	25	4
	Cherry Bomb	11/28/87	1/9/88	7	10
Cover Girls					
	Because Of You	2/6/88	3/12/88	15	8
	We Can't Go Wrong	1/6/90	2/3/90	10	14
Cray, Robert, Band					
	Smoking Gun	3/14/87	4/18/87	9	6
Crosby, Stills & Nash					
	Wasted On The Way	7/24/82	9/4/82	14	15
	Southern Cross	10/9/82	12/4/82	22	18
also see Nash, Graham					
Cross, Christopher					
	Ride Like The Wind	3/29/80	5/17/80	2	25
	Sailing	8/2/80	9/6/80	2	20
	Never Be The Same	10/11/80	11/22/80	20	19
	Arthur's Theme (Best That You Can Do)	9/5/81	10/17/81	3	21
	All Right	2/12/83	3/5/83	16	13
	Think Of Laura	1/14/84	2/11/84	8	13
Crowded House					
	Don't Dream It's Over	1/17/87	4/25/87	1	20
	Something So Strong	7/4/87	7/25/87	21	5
Culture Club					
	Do You Really Want To Hurt Me	1/29/83	3/5/83	3	20

Artist	Title	Debut	Peak	Pos	Wks
	Time (Clock Of The Heart)	5/21/83	6/18/83	7	17
	I'll Tumble 4 Ya	8/13/83	9/17/83	13	13
	Church Of The Poison Mind	11/5/83	12/3/83	11	17
	Karma Chameleon	12/24/83	2/4/84	1	20
	Miss Me Blind	3/10/84	5/5/84	9	16
	It's A Miracle	5/26/84	6/23/84	20	9
	Move Away	4/5/86	5/3/86	22	11

Cure

	Just Like Heaven	12/12/87	1/9/88	21	6
	Love Song	9/9/89	10/28/89	2	14

Cutting Crew

	(I Just) Died In Your Arms	3/21/87	5/2/87	1	17
	I've Been In Love Before	9/5/87	11/21/87	10	13

Dahl, Steve & Teenage Radiation

	Do You Think I'm Disco	9/8/79	10/6/79	5	19
	Ayatollah	1/26/80	2/9/80	12	16

Daltrey, Roger

	Without Your Love	1/17/81	3/7/81	37	15
	After The Fire	11/9/85	11/23/85	30	5

also see the Who

Damian, Michael

	Rock On	4/1/89	6/24/89	1	20
	Was It Nothing At All	12/30/89	2/10/90	4	13

Daniels, Charlie, Band

	The Devil Went Down To Georgia	8/11/79	9/22/79	2	23
	In America	7/12/80	8/23/80	8	19
	The Legend Of Wooley Swamp	8/23/80	9/27/80	10	19
	Still In Saigon	4/24/82	5/22/82	16	11

Danny Wilson

	Mary's Prayer	7/18/87	8/29/87	8	11

D'Arby, Terence Trent

	Wishing Well	4/9/88	5/7/88	3	13
	Sign Your Name	7/23/88	8/20/88	10	8
	Dance Little Sister (Part One)	9/24/88	10/22/88	15	6

Artist Title	Debut	Peak	Pos	Wks
David & David				
Welcome To The Boomtown	10/11/86	11/15/86	20	12
Davis, Mac				
It's Hard To Be Humble	5/3/80	5/24/80	15	18
Davis, Paul				
Cool Night	1/16/82	2/27/82	17	14
'65 Love Affair	4/17/82	6/5/82	2	19
Dayne, Taylor				
Tell It To My Heart	1/2/88	1/23/88	12	10
Prove Your Love	4/23/88	5/21/88	15	8
I'll Always Love You	9/17/88	10/29/88	6	9
Don't Rush Me	12/10/88	1/28/89	3	11
With Every Beat Of My Heart	11/18/89	12/16/89	7	10
Love Will Lead You Back	3/31/90	4/28/90	7	6
Dazz Band				
Let It Whip	7/10/82	8/21/82	7	16
Dead Or Alive				
You Spin Me Round (Like A Record)	7/6/85	8/24/85	14	13
Brand New Lover	1/17/87	3/14/87	3	12
DeBarge				
Rhythm Of The Night	3/30/85	4/27/85	3	15
Who's Holding Donna Now	7/6/85	8/31/85	8	15
DeBarge, Chico				
Talk To Me	1/17/87	2/14/87	21	7
DeBarge, El with DeBarge				
You Wear It Well	9/28/85	11/9/85	37	8
Debarge, El				
Who's Johnny	5/10/86	6/28/86	6	15
DeBurgh, Chris				
Don't Pay The Ferryman	5/28/83	6/25/83	23	10
High On Emotion	8/25/84	9/15/84	27	7
The Lady In Red	3/28/87	5/30/87	2	18

Artist	Title	Debut	Peak	Pos	Wks
Deele					
	Two Occasions	4/23/88	5/28/88	7	7
	also see Babyface				
Def Leppard					
	Photograph	3/26/83	5/14/83	7	21
	Rock Of Ages	6/25/83	8/6/83	6	19
	Foolin'	9/24/83	10/29/83	15	14
	Animal	10/17/87	12/12/87	12	11
	Hysteria	2/20/88	3/19/88	16	7
	Pour Some Sugar On Me	5/7/88	7/16/88	1	19
	Love Bites	9/3/88	10/8/88	1	13
	Armageddon It	11/19/88	12/31/88	5	13
	Rocket	3/18/89	4/29/89	8	8
	Excitable	4/22/89	6/3/89	16	7
Depeche Mode					
	People Are People	6/29/85	8/3/85	10	13
	Route 66	6/3/89	7/15/89	7	9
	also see Erasure				
DeSario, Teri with KC					
	Yes, I'm Ready	1/19/80	3/8/80	5	16
	also see KC & the Sunshine Band				
Devo					
	Whip It	11/8/80	12/20/80	2	36
	Working In The Coal Mine	10/3/81	10/24/81	13	12
Dexys Midnight Runners					
	Come On Eileen	'2/12/83	4/9/83	3	20
DeYoung, Dennis					
	Desert Moon	9/15/84	10/27/84	15	15
	Call Me	3/15/86	4/19/86	44	7
	This Is The Time	6/21/86	7/5/86	46	4
	also see Styx				
Diamond, Neil					
	September Morn'	2/9/80	3/15/80	17	14
	Love On The Rocks	11/1/80	1/10/81	8	22
	Hello Again	2/28/81	4/11/81	12	13

Artist	Title	Debut	Peak	Pos	Wks
	America	5/23/81	6/20/81	24	10
	Yesterday's Songs	12/5/81	12/26/81	20	10
	Heartlight	10/16/82	11/6/82	7	15
	Headed For The Future	6/7/86	6/28/86	45	5
Diesel					
	Sausalito Summernight	10/31/81	12/5/81	18	11
Dino					
	I Like It	7/15/89	8/19/89	4	11
Dire Straits					
	Money For Nothing	7/20/85	8/31/85	1	20
	Walk Of Life	11/2/85	12/21/85	25	16
	So Far Away	3/8/86	4/5/86	24	9
Dirt Band					
	An American Dream	3/15/80	4/5/80	25	9
D.J. Jazzy Jeff & the Fresh Prince					
	Parents Just Don't Understand	7/9/88	8/13/88	3	9
	A Nightmare On My Street	8/20/88	9/24/88	2	8
D-Mob					
	C'mon And Get My Love	3/3/90	3/31/90	7	10
Dolby, Thomas					
	She Blinded Me With Science	5/7/83	5/28/83	4	16
	Airhead	7/2/88	7/16/88	25	4
Doobie Brothers					
	Real Love	9/6/80	10/25/80	8	20
	One Step Closer	12/20/80	1/24/81	35	8

also see McDonald, Michael and Simmons, Patrick

Artist	Title	Debut	Peak	Pos	Wks
Dore, Charlie					
	Pilot Of The Airwaves	5/10/80	5/31/80	20	12
Double					
	The Captain Of Her Heart	8/16/86	9/27/86	14	12
Dr. Hook					
	Sexy Eyes	4/19/80	6/14/80	10	20

Artist	Title	Debut	Peak	Pos	Wks
Dream Academy					
	Life In A Northern Town	12/14/85	2/8/86	9	17
	The Love Parade	5/3/86	5/17/86	40	6
Dupree, Robbie					
	Steal Away	6/7/80	7/19/80	4	20
	Hot Rod Hearts	10/4/80	10/25/80	31	8
Duran Duran					
	Hungry Like The Wolf	2/5/83	3/5/83	2	20
	Is There Something I Should Know	6/25/83	8/27/83	18	16
	Union Of The Snake	12/3/83	1/14/84	7	15
	New Moon On Monday	2/4/84	3/17/84	11	17
	The Reflex	5/12/84	6/16/84	1	18
	The Wild Boys	11/3/84	12/8/84	4	17
	Save A Prayer	2/2/85	2/23/85	22	11
	A View To A Kill	5/18/85	7/13/85	1	17
	Notorious	11/15/86	1/17/87	2	13
	I Don't Want Your Love	10/15/88	11/26/88	8	9
	All She Wants Is	12/31/88	2/4/89	9	8

also see Arcadia and the Power Station

Artist	Title	Debut	Peak	Pos	Wks
Eagles					
	Heartache Tonight	9/29/79	11/17/79	4	22
	The Long Run	12/15/79	2/2/80	14	14
	I Can't Tell You Why	3/1/80	5/3/80	11	20

also see Felder, Don; Frey, Glenn; Henley, Don; Meisner, Randy; Schmit, Timothy B. and Walsh, Joe

Artist	Title	Debut	Peak	Pos	Wks
Earth, Wind & Fire					
	Let's Groove	12/19/81	1/30/82	9	15

also see Bailey Philip with Phil Collins

Artist	Title	Debut	Peak	Pos	Wks
Easton, Sheena					
	Morning Train (Nine To Five)	3/28/81	5/2/81	1	22
	Modern Girl	6/6/81	7/25/81	18	15
	For Your Eyes Only	8/22/81	10/24/81	6	24
	Telefone (Long Distance Love Affair)	11/19/83	12/10/83	20	9
	Strut	10/20/84	12/1/84	3	17
	Sugar Walls	2/2/85	3/2/85	11	11
	Do It For Love	10/26/85	12/7/85	33	10

Artist	Title	Debut	Peak	Pos	Wks
	So Far So Good	7/19/86	9/27/86	31	13

also see Rogers, Kenny & Sheena Easton

Edelweiss
	Bring Me Edelweiss	5/27/89	7/8/89	5	10

Edmunds, Dave
	Slipping Away	7/2/83	7/23/83	25	12

Electric Light Orchestra
	Don't Bring Me Down	8/4/79	10/13/79	5	24
	I'm Alive	7/5/80	8/9/80	25	17
	All Over The World	8/9/80	10/11/80	6	17
	Hold On Tight	9/5/81	9/26/81	19	13
	Rock 'N' Roll Is King	8/6/83	9/10/83	8	13
	Calling America	2/15/86	3/29/86	22	12

also see Newton-John, Olivia and Traveling Wilburys

Erasure
	Chains Of Love	8/6/88	9/3/88	19	5
	Chains Of Love	10/22/88	11/5/88	16	3
	A Little Respect	1/7/89	2/18/89	5	10

also see Depeche Mode

Escape Club
	Wild, Wild West	9/17/88	11/26/88	4	16

Estefan, Gloria
	Don't Wanna Lose You	8/12/89	9/16/89	3	10
	Get On Your Feet	11/4/89	12/2/89	13	11
	Here We Are	1/27/90	3/3/90	14	11

also see Miami Sound Machine

Estus, Deon with George Michael
	Heaven Help Me	4/8/89	4/22/89	16	5

also see Michael, George and Wham!

Europe
	The Final Countdown	1/31/87	4/4/87	9	11
	Rock The Night	5/9/87	6/27/87	23	9
	Carrie	8/22/87	10/3/87	5	13

Eurythmics
	Sweet Dreams (Are Made Of This)	7/23/83	9/3/83	1	19

Artist	Title	Debut	Peak	Pos	Wks
	Here Comes The Rain Again	2/25/84	3/17/84	10	16
	Who's That Girl	6/16/84	7/7/84	29	7
	Right By Your Side	9/15/84	9/22/84	34	5
	Would I Lie To You	5/25/85	7/13/85	13	14
	There Must Be An Angel (Playing With My Heart)	8/31/85	9/21/85	30	7
	Missionary Man	7/26/86	9/20/86	13	13

also see Lennox, Annie & Al Green

Expose

	Come Go With Me	2/28/87	4/11/87	2	8
	Point Of No Return	5/23/87	7/18/87	7	15
	Let Me Be The One	8/22/87	10/17/87	17	13
	Seasons Change	2/20/88	3/5/88	12	9
	What You Don't Know	6/10/89	7/1/89	17	5

Fabulous Thunderbirds

	Tuff Enuff	5/24/86	7/12/86	12	12

Fagen, Donald

	I.G.Y. (What A Beautiful World)	10/23/82	11/13/82	14	14

also see Steely Dan

Falco

	Rock Me Amadeus	2/15/86	3/29/86	1	17

Faltermeyer, Harold

	Axel F	4/6/85	6/1/85	1	20

Fat Boys & the Beach Boys

	Wipeout	8/29/87	9/26/87	8	12

Fat Boys with Chubby Checker

	The Twist (Yo, Twist)	7/2/88	7/16/88	20	4

also see the Beach Boys

Felder, Don

	Heavy Metal (Takin' A Ride)	10/3/81	10/24/81	22	11

also see the Eagles

Fine Young Cannibals

	She Drives Me Crazy	1/28/89	3/18/89	5	14
	Good Thing	4/22/89	7/1/89	2	20

Artist	Title	Debut	Peak	Pos	Wks
Firm					
	Radioactive	4/13/85	5/4/85	24	8
	All The Kings Horses	3/8/86	3/29/86	38	5
also see the Honeydrippers					
Fixx					
	Saved By Zero	7/23/83	8/13/83	21	15
	One Thing Leads To Another	9/17/83	10/29/83	11	20
	The Sign Of Fire	1/21/84	2/4/84	39	5
	Are We Ourselves	8/25/84	10/20/84	8	14
	Secret Separation	6/7/86	7/26/86	16	12
	Driven Out	2/25/89	3/18/89	23	4
Flack, Roberta					
	Making Love	5/29/82	6/19/82	20	11
also see Bryson, Peabo & Roberta Flack					
Fleetwood Mac					
	Tusk	9/29/79	11/10/79	6	20
	Sara	1/19/80	2/9/80	10	13
	Hold Me	7/3/82	8/14/82	5	19
	Gypsy	10/16/82	11/6/82	13	10
	Love In Store	12/18/82	1/15/83	31	9
	Big Love	3/28/87	5/16/87	9	11
	Little Lies	8/29/87	10/31/87	7	14
also see Buckingham, Lindsey; McVie, Christine and Nicks, Stevie					
Flesh For Lulu					
	I Go Crazy	3/14/87	4/18/87	19	6
Flock Of Seagulls					
	I Ran (So Far Away)	9/18/82	10/30/82	5	18
	Space Age Love Song	12/25/82	1/29/83	18	12
Flying Lizards					
	Money	1/12/80	2/9/80	18	11
Fogelberg, Dan					
	Longer	1/26/80	3/15/80	3	19
	Heart Hotels	5/17/80	6/7/80	30	10
	Hard To Say	9/12/81	10/24/81	18	19
	Leader Of The Band	2/6/82	3/6/82	15	15

Artist	Title	Debut	Peak	Pos	Wks
	Run For The Roses	5/29/82	6/26/82	31	9
	The Language Of Love	2/25/84	3/24/84	18	11
Fogerty, John					
	The Old Man Down The Road	2/9/85	3/9/85	17	11
	Rock And Roll Girls	4/6/85	5/11/85	15	13
	/Centerfield	5/25/85	6/22/85	37	9
	Change In The Weather	11/15/86	11/22/86	46	4
Forbert, Steve					
	Romeo's Tune	2/9/80	3/15/80	12	13
Force M.D.'s					
	Tender Love	4/12/86	4/26/86	19	7
Ford, Lita					
	Kiss Me Deadly	4/2/88	6/4/88	3	17
Foreigner					
	Head Games	12/1/79	1/12/80	16	12
	Urgent	7/4/81	9/26/81	2	30
	Waiting For A Girl Like You	10/10/81	11/21/81	3	23
	Juke Box Hero	3/6/82	4/3/82	14	11
	I Want To Know What Love Is	12/22/84	2/9/85	3	20
	That Was Yesterday	3/16/85	5/4/85	20	13
	Say You Will	1/30/88	2/20/88	14	5
	also see Gramm, Lou					
Four Tops					
	When She Was My Girl	10/10/81	11/14/81	13	14
Fox, Samantha					
	Touch Me (I Want Your Body)	1/17/87	2/14/87	5	9
	Naughty Girls (Need Love Too)	4/23/88	6/4/88	2	15
	I Wanna Have Some Fun	12/3/88	1/21/89	2	12
	I Only Wanna Be With You	5/13/89	5/20/89	21	2
Frampton, Peter					
	Lying	2/8/86	3/29/86	46	8
Franke & the Knockouts					
	Sweetheart	5/23/81	7/25/81	16	16
	Without You (Not Another Lonely Night)	4/10/82	6/12/82	18	20

Artist Title	Debut	Peak	Pos	Wks
Frankie Goes To Hollywood				
Relax	1/26/85	3/23/85	7	17
Franklin, Aretha				
Freeway Of Love	7/27/85	9/21/85	4	15
Who's Zoomin' Who	10/12/85	11/30/85	8	17
Another Night	1/18/86	3/29/86	23	14
Jumpin' Jack Flash	9/27/86	11/8/86	10	12
Franklin, Aretha & George Michael				
I Knew You Were Waiting (For Me)	3/7/87	4/25/87	3	15
also see Michael, George and Wham!				
Frey, Glenn				
The One You Love	10/9/82	11/6/82	12	15
Sexy Girl	7/28/84	9/1/84	13	10
The Heat Is On	1/19/85	3/16/85	1	22
Smuggler's Blues	5/18/85	6/29/85	10	13
You Belong To The City	9/14/85	11/23/85	1	19
True Love	8/27/88	9/17/88	23	5
also see the Eagles				
Frida				
I Know There's Something Going On	3/12/83	4/16/83	7	14
also see ABBA				
Gabriel, Peter				
Games Without Frontiers	7/26/80	9/6/80	5	18
Shock The Monkey	11/20/82	12/25/82	14	15
Sledgehammer	6/7/86	7/19/86	2	16
In Your Eyes	9/13/86	10/4/86	26	10
Big Time	11/22/86	3/14/87	6	19
In Your Eyes	5/20/89	7/8/89	3	14
Gabriel, Peter & Kate Bush				
Don't Give Up	4/18/87	4/25/87	36	3
also see Genesis				
Gaye, Marvin				
Sexual Healing	12/11/82	1/15/83	11	18
Gayle, Crystal				
Half The Way	12/8/79	12/29/79	22	10
also see Rabbitt, Eddie with Crystal Gayle				

Artist	Title	Debut	Peak	Pos	Wks

Geils, J., Band
	Love Stinks	5/24/80	7/5/80	15	13
	Centerfold	12/5/81	1/16/82	1	27
	Freeze-Frame	3/20/82	4/17/82	3	20
	I Do	1/15/83	1/29/83	29	9

also see Wolf, Peter

Geldof, Bob
| | Love Like A Rocket | 2/21/87 | 3/14/87 | 32 | 5 |

also see Band Aid

General Public
| | Tenderness | 3/2/85 | 3/9/85 | 33 | 6 |

Genesis
	Misunderstanding	6/21/80	8/2/80	4	19
	Turn It On Again	10/11/80	11/1/80	31	10
	Abacab	9/12/81	9/12/81	49	1
	No Reply At All	10/24/81	11/21/81	11	17
	Abacab	12/19/81	1/30/82	14	14
	Man On The Corner	3/27/82	5/8/82	23	15
	Paperlate	6/5/82	7/10/82	11	15
	That's All	12/10/83	1/21/84	13	17
	Taking It All Too Hard	6/16/84	7/14/84	34	8
	Invisible Touch	5/31/86	7/5/86	5	16
	Throwing It All Away	8/16/86	10/25/86	14	15
	Land Of Confusion	11/1/86	1/31/87	8	16
	Tonight, Tonight, Tonight	2/14/87	4/4/87	3	9
	In Too Deep	4/25/87	6/13/87	8	13

also see Collins, Phil; Gabriel, Peter; GTR and Mike + the Mechanics

Georgia Satellites
	Keep Your Hands To Yourself	11/15/86	2/7/87	1	19
	Battleship Chains	1/24/87	3/28/87	20	10
	Hippy Hippy Shake	10/8/88	11/12/88	19	7

Gibb, Andy
| | Desire | 2/23/80 | 3/22/80 | 24 | 10 |
| | Time Is Time | 1/17/81 | 2/7/81 | 31 | 8 |

Artist	Title	Debut	Peak	Pos	Wks
Gibb, Andy & Olivia Newton-John					
	I Can't Help It	5/17/80	6/7/80	27	7
also see Newton-John, Olivia					
Gibb, Barry					
	Shine Shine	9/29/84	10/13/84	28	5
also see Streisand, Barbra & Barry Gibb					
Gibson, Debbie					
	Only In My Dreams	5/30/87	9/5/87	3	27
	Shake Your Love	10/31/87	12/26/87	5	15
	Out Of The Blue	2/13/88	4/9/88	2	16
	Foolish Beat	6/4/88	7/2/88	2	11
	Lost In Your Eyes	1/28/89	3/18/89	1	14
	Electric Youth	4/8/89	5/13/89	5	8
Giuffria					
	Call To The Heart	1/5/85	2/9/85	11	11
Glass Tiger					
	Don't Forget Me (When I'm Gone)	8/2/86	10/25/86	5	18
	Someday	11/22/86	1/24/87	10	12
	I Will Be There	3/14/87	4/11/87	26	5
Go West					
	Don't Look Down - The Sequel	10/3/87	10/3/87	41	1
Godley & Creme					
	Cry	8/24/85	9/21/85	13	12
Go-Go's					
	Our Lips Are Sealed	12/26/81	2/13/82	2	25
	We Got The Beat	2/27/82	4/3/82	2	21
	Vacation	7/24/82	8/21/82	6	14
	Head Over Heels	4/14/84	5/19/84	19	13
also see Carlisle, Belinda and Wiedlin, Jane					
Golden Earring					
	Twilight Zone	3/5/83	4/16/83	4	18
Graham, Larry					
	One In A Million You	8/9/80	8/30/80	24	14

Artist Title	Debut	Peak	Pos	Wks
Gramm, Lou				
Just Between You And Me	11/25/89	2/10/90	3	19
also see Foreigner				
Grandmaster Flash & Melle Mel				
White Lines (Don't Don't Do It)	1/7/84	2/11/84	31	15
Grant, Eddy				
Electric Avenue	6/4/83	7/9/83	1	19
Grateful Dead				
Touch Of Grey	7/25/87	9/12/87	8	10
Great White				
Once Bitten Twice Shy	6/17/89	7/22/89	1	14
GTR				
When The Heart Rules The Mind	6/7/86	7/19/86	18	12
also see Asia, Genesis and Yes				
Guns N' Roses				
Sweet Child O' Mine	7/30/88	9/10/88	1	13
Welcome To The Jungle	10/29/88	12/31/88	2	16
Paradise City	1/14/89	3/11/89	4	16
Patience	3/18/89	5/27/89	1	21
Nightrain	5/13/89	6/3/89	18	5
Hagar, Sammy				
I'll Fall In Love Again	1/30/82	3/6/82	30	12
Your Love Is Driving Me Crazy	1/8/83	1/29/83	23	13
Never Give Up	4/9/83	5/7/83	35	7
I Can't Drive 55	11/10/84	12/8/84	21	10
Give To Live	7/18/87	8/29/87	16	8
also see Van Halen				
Hall, Daryl				
Dreamtime	8/2/86	10/4/86	20	13
Foolish Pride	11/1/86	11/29/86	41	6
Hall, Daryl & John Oates				
You've Lost That Lovin' Feeling	11/22/80	12/20/80	19	15
Kiss On My List	3/21/81	5/9/81	3	19
You Make My Dreams	7/18/81	8/8/81	24	11
Private Eyes	9/5/81	11/7/81	1	29

Artist	Title	Debut	Peak	Pos	Wks
	I Can't Go For That (No Can Do)	12/19/81	1/30/82	2	20
	Maneater	11/13/82	1/8/83	2	21
	One On One	3/5/83	3/26/83	11	15
	Family Man	5/28/83	7/16/83	9	14
	Say It Isn't So	11/19/83	1/14/84	9	16
	Adult Education	2/18/84	3/24/84	19	15
	Out Of Touch	10/13/84	11/24/84	8	18
	Method Of Modern Love	12/22/84	2/2/85	15	17
	Some Things Are Better Left Unsaid	3/23/85	4/27/85	28	10

Hall, John, Band

	Crazy (Keep On Falling)	1/30/82	3/6/82	18	11

Hallyday, David

	He's My Girl	8/1/87	9/5/87	35	9

Hammer, Jan

	Miami Vice Theme	9/21/85	10/26/85	1	20

Hardcastle, Paul

	19	6/1/85	6/29/85	8	13

Harnen, Jimmy with Synch

	Where Are You Now	5/6/89	6/24/89	7	10

Harrison, George

	All Those Years Ago	5/23/81	6/20/81	3	14
	Got My Mind Set On You	11/7/87	1/2/88	1	19

also see the Beatles and the Traveling Wilburys

Harry, Debbie

	French Kissin	12/13/86	1/17/87	22	9

also see Blondie

Hart, Corey

	Sunglasses At Night	8/4/84	9/8/84	5	13
	It Ain't Enough	10/27/84	12/8/84	27	12
	Never Surrender	6/8/85	8/3/85	3	18
	Boy In The Box	9/14/85	11/2/85	21	12
	Everything In My Heart	11/30/85	2/8/86	37	12
	I Am By Your Side	9/20/86	11/15/86	34	11
	Can't Help Falling In Love	12/20/86	2/14/87	20	11

Artist Title	Debut	Peak	Pos	Wks
Hartman, Dan				
I Can Dream About You	6/16/84	8/25/84	5	18
We Are The Young	11/3/84	12/15/84	17	12
Hayes, Isaac				
Don't Let Go	12/1/79	12/29/79	18	15
Head, Murray				
One Night In Bangkok	3/16/85	4/27/85	5	17
Healey, Jeff, Band				
Angel Eyes	8/19/89	9/30/89	3	12
Heart				
Even It Up	2/9/80	3/15/80	21	15
Tell It Like It Is	12/13/80	1/24/81	19	13
What About Love	7/20/85	8/31/85	16	14
Never	9/28/85	12/7/85	10	17
These Dreams	1/18/86	3/29/86	7	17
Nothin' At All	4/26/86	5/31/86	19	12
Alone	5/30/87	7/18/87	1	20
All I Wanna Do Is Make Love To You	4/21/90	5/5/90	13	3
also see Reno, Mike & Ann Wilson and Wilson, Ann & Robin Zander				
Henley, Don				
Dirty Laundry	10/30/82	12/4/82	3	21
The Boys Of Summer	1/12/85	2/2/85	9	12
All She Wants To Do Is Dance	3/2/85	4/20/85	13	16
Sunset Grill	9/7/85	10/5/85	26	10
The End Of The Innocence	7/22/89	8/26/89	7	7
The Last Worthless Evening	11/18/89	12/16/89	14	7
also see the Eagles and Nicks, Stevie with Don Henley				
Higgins, Bertie				
Key Largo	4/3/82	5/15/82	4	17
Hill, Dan with Vonda Sheppard				
Can't We Try	8/15/87	9/19/87	12	12
Hodgson, Roger				
Had A Dream (Sleeping With The Enemy)	10/20/84	12/15/84	16	15
also see Supertramp				

Artist Title	Debut	Peak	Pos	Wks
Hollies				
Stop In The Name Of Love	8/20/83	8/20/83	39	5
Holmes, Rupert				
Escape (The Pina Colada Song)	12/1/79	1/12/80	1	20
Him	3/8/80	4/12/80	8	15
Honeydrippers				
Sea Of Love	11/10/84	12/22/84	4	16
Rockin' At Midnight	2/2/85	2/16/85	27	7
also see the Firm and Plant, Robert				
Honeymoon Suite				
Feel It Again	3/8/86	4/19/86	37	9
Hooters				
And We Danced	9/28/85	11/2/85	14	11
Day By Day	2/1/86	3/1/86	34	7
Where Do The Children Go	4/5/86	5/17/86	39	7
also see Lauper, Cyndi				
Hornsby, Bruce & the Range				
The Way It Is	10/11/86	12/13/86	5	15
Mandolin Rain	2/28/87	3/28/87	14	7
Every Little Kiss	5/23/87	6/27/87	26	7
Houston, Whitney				
You Give Good Love	7/6/85	8/10/85	7	19
Saving All My Love For You	9/21/85	11/9/85	2	15
How Will I Know	12/14/85	3/1/86	1	22
Greatest Love Of All	3/29/86	5/24/86	1	17
I Wanna Dance With Somebody (Who Loves Me)	5/16/87	6/27/87	1	18
Didn't We Almost Have It All	8/15/87	9/26/87	2	16
So Emotional	10/24/87	12/5/87	11	13
Where Do Broken Hearts Go	4/2/88	4/30/88	5	9
Love Will Save The Day	7/23/88	8/20/88	14	5
One Moment In Time	9/24/88	11/12/88	6	11
Human League				
Don't You Want Me	4/24/82	6/26/82	1	25
Human	9/27/86	11/15/86	2	17

Artist Title	Debut	Peak	Pos	Wks
Hunter, John				
Tragedy	2/2/85	2/23/85	33	8
Icehouse				
Crazy	11/14/87	12/12/87	21	5
Idol, Billy				
White Wedding	7/2/83	7/30/83	8	14
Eyes Without A Face	6/9/84	7/14/84	5	15
To Be A Lover	10/25/86	11/22/86	12	13
Don't Need A Gun	1/17/87	2/14/87	35	5
Mony Mony "Live"	9/5/87	11/21/87	1	22
Iglesias, Julio & Willie Nelson				
To All The Girls I've Loved Before	3/31/84	5/19/84	2	23
Iglesias, Julio & Diana Ross				
All Of You	7/28/84	8/18/84	11	14
also see Nelson, Willie and Ross, Diana				
Information Society				
What's On Your Mind (Pure Energy)	9/3/88	10/22/88	8	11
Walking Away	12/24/88	1/21/89	15	6
Ingram, James with Michael McDonald				
Yah Mo B There	12/24/83	2/18/84	19	16
also see Austin, Patti; McDonald, Michael; Rogers, Kenny and Ronstadt, Linda				
Inner City				
Big Fun	12/17/88	1/21/89	8	9
INXS				
The One Thing	6/4/83	6/18/83	29	8
What You Need	2/1/86	4/5/86	7	17
Need You Tonight	10/24/87	12/19/87	7	17
Devil Inside	3/26/88	4/23/88	6	10
New Sensation	6/4/88	7/16/88	5	8
Never Tear Us Apart	9/17/88	10/15/88	13	5
INXS & Jimmy Barnes				
Good Times	7/4/87	7/18/87	34	5
Iris, Donnie				
Ah! Leah!	2/7/81	4/4/81	7	17

Artist	Title	Debut	Peak	Pos	Wks
	Love Is Like A Rock	12/26/81	2/20/82	5	17
	My Girl	4/17/82	5/22/82	33	12

Jackson, Freddie

	You Are My Lady	10/19/85	11/30/85	6	17
	He'll Never Love You (Like I Do)	2/8/86	2/22/86	31	6

Jackson, Janet

	What Have You Done For Me Lately	4/19/86	5/17/86	7	14
	Nasty	6/7/86	7/12/86	3	15
	When I Think Of You	8/16/86	10/18/86	3	18
	Control	11/22/86	1/24/87	6	13
	Let's Wait Awhile	2/14/87	3/21/87	4	9
	The Pleasure Principle	7/11/87	8/8/87	14	9
	Miss You Much	9/2/89	10/21/89	1	16
	Rhythm Nation	12/2/89	1/13/90	9	13
	Escapade	1/27/90	3/17/90	1	15
	Alright	4/14/90	5/5/90	9	4

Jackson, Jermaine

	Let's Get Serious	5/31/80	7/5/80	19	13
	Tell Me I'm Not Dreamin' (Too Good To Be True)	5/5/84	5/5/84	46	2
	Dynamite	9/1/84	9/29/84	12	12
	Do What You Do	1/19/85	2/9/85	20	9
	I Think It's Love	3/1/86	4/19/86	26	13

also see the Jacksons

Jackson, Joe

	Steppin' Out	10/9/82	11/13/82	2	18
	Breaking Us In Two	2/19/83	3/19/83	22	11
	You Can't Get What You Want (Till You Know What You Want)	6/2/84	6/30/84	18	10
	Right And Wrong	5/17/86	6/14/86	28	8

Jackson, Michael

	Don't Stop 'Til You Get Enough	9/29/79	10/27/79	7	20
	Rock With You	12/29/79	2/9/80	1	24
	Off The Wall	4/5/80	5/3/80	21	13
	Billie Jean	2/12/83	3/26/83	1	29
	Beat It	4/2/83	5/7/83	1	25
	Wanna Be Startin' Somethin'	7/9/83	8/6/83	5	14

Artist	Title	Debut	Peak	Pos	Wks
	Human Nature	8/20/83	9/10/83	21	13
	P.Y.T. (Pretty Young Thing)	11/26/83	12/24/83	16	17
	Thriller	1/14/84	3/10/84	5	21
	I Just Can't Stop Loving You	8/15/87	9/19/87	3	15
	Bad	9/12/87	11/7/87	8	13
	The Way You Make Me Feel	11/21/87	1/16/88	3	15
	Man In The Mirror	3/5/88	4/9/88	1	11
	Dirty Diana	5/7/88	6/25/88	1	15
	Another Part Of Me	9/17/88	10/1/88	25	4
	Smooth Criminal	12/17/88	1/14/89	9	7

Jackson, Michael & Paul McCartney

Artist	Title	Debut	Peak	Pos	Wks
	The Girl Is Mine	11/27/82	12/25/82	7	13

also see McCartney, Paul & Michael Jackson

Jacksons

Artist	Title	Debut	Peak	Pos	Wks
	Lovely One	11/29/80	12/6/80	33	8
	State Of Shock	6/30/84	8/4/84	6	13

also see Jackson, Jermaine

Jagger, Mick

Artist	Title	Debut	Peak	Pos	Wks
	Just Another Night	2/9/85	3/23/85	19	13

Jagger, Mick & David Bowie

Artist	Title	Debut	Peak	Pos	Wks
	Dancing In The Street	8/31/85	9/28/85	4	15

also see Bowie, David and the Rolling Stones

James, Rick

Artist	Title	Debut	Peak	Pos	Wks
	17	9/1/84	9/15/84	29	6

Jarreau, Al

Artist	Title	Debut	Peak	Pos	Wks
	We're In This Love Together	10/24/81	11/21/81	12	10
	Moonlighting	6/13/87	7/25/87	17	10

Jefferson Starship

Artist	Title	Debut	Peak	Pos	Wks
	Jane	12/8/79	1/19/80	6	16
	Find Your Way Back	4/11/81	6/6/81	15	17
	Stranger	8/8/81	9/5/81	37	7
	Be My Lady	11/6/82	11/27/82	30	10
	Can't Find Love	5/14/83	6/11/83	36	8
	No Way Out	6/23/84	7/21/84	25	10
	Layin' It On The Line	9/15/84	9/29/84	38	5

Artist Title	Debut	Peak	Pos	Wks
Starship				
We Built This City	9/14/85	11/30/85	3	22
Sara	1/11/86	3/15/86	5	16
Tomorrow Doesn't Matter Tonight	4/5/86	5/10/86	36	10
Nothing's Gonna Stop Us Now	2/7/87	4/11/87	1	16
It's Not Over ('Til It's Over)	8/8/87	8/29/87	30	5
also see Balin, Marty and the KBC Band				
Jellybean				
Sidewalk Talk	11/23/85	1/18/86	19	16
Jennings, Waylon				
Theme From The Dukes Of Hazzard (Good Ol' Boys)	11/22/80	12/20/80	17	18
Jets				
Crush On You	5/17/86	6/28/86	2	13
Private Number	8/9/86	9/20/86	36	8
You Got It All	2/7/87	3/14/87	10	8
Cross My Broken Heart	5/30/87	8/1/87	19	12
I Do You	10/31/87	12/5/87	21	6
Rocket 2 U	2/27/88	4/16/88	3	11
Make It Real	5/14/88	7/2/88	5	12
also see Boys Club				
Jett, Joan & the Blackhearts				
I Love Rock 'N Roll	2/6/82	3/13/82	1	28
Crimson And Clover	5/22/82	6/12/82	14	15
Do You Wanna Touch Me (Oh Yeah)	9/11/82	10/16/82	11	13
Good Music	11/8/86	11/22/86	47	6
Roadrunner (Radio On)	12/20/86	1/24/87	34	6
/Light Of Day *(as the Barbusters)*	2/21/87	3/28/87	23	7
I Hate Myself For Loving You	9/3/88	10/1/88	3	8
Little Liar	12/24/88	1/21/89	17	5
Jive Bunny & the Mastermixers				
Swing The Mood	9/23/89	11/4/89	1	9
J.J. Fad				
Supersonic	4/9/88	5/28/88	12	9
Billy Joel				
You May Be Right	3/22/80	5/17/80	10	28

Artist	Title	Debut	Peak	Pos	Wks
	It's Still Rock And Roll To Me	5/31/80	7/26/80	1	24
	Don't Ask Me Why	8/2/80	9/13/80	21	14
	Sometimes A Fantasy	10/11/80	11/15/80	25	11
	Say Goodbye To Hollywood	9/12/81	10/24/81	20	15
	Pressure	10/16/82	11/13/82	12	15
	Allentown	1/22/83	2/19/83	17	14
	Tell Her About It	8/13/83	10/8/83	5	20
	Uptown Girl	10/22/83	12/3/83	4	22
	The Longest Time	5/12/84	6/16/84	6	15
	Leave A Tender Moment Alone	8/11/84	8/25/84	31	10
	Keeping The Faith	2/2/85	3/16/85	26	15
	You're Only Human (Second Wind)	7/20/85	9/21/85	15	15
	The Night Is Still Young	10/26/85	12/7/85	41	7
	Modern Woman	6/7/86	7/12/86	19	12
	A Matter Of Trust	8/9/86	10/11/86	34	14
	This Is The Time	12/13/86	1/10/87	42	5
	We Didn't Start The Fire	11/11/89	1/6/90	1	19
	I Go To Extremes	1/20/90	3/3/90	12	12

John, Elton

	Little Jeannie	6/7/80	7/19/80	8	17
	I'm Still Standing	6/18/83	7/9/83	17	15
	I Guess That's Why They Call It The Blues	1/7/84	2/4/84	3	14
	Sad Songs (Say So Much)	6/23/84	7/28/84	9	14
	Who Wears These Shoes	9/22/84	10/20/84	29	10
	Wrap Her Up	11/2/85	12/14/85	22	11
	Nikita	1/18/86	3/29/86	15	17
	Candle In The Wind	11/28/87	1/16/88	9	9
	I Don't Wanna Go On With You Like That	7/9/88	8/13/88	9	7
	Pinball Wizard	8/12/89	8/26/89	24	3
	Sacrifice	2/17/90	3/17/90	6	12

also see (Warwick), Dionne & Friends

John, Robert

	Sad Eyes	8/18/79	9/29/79	2	24

Johnny Hates Jazz

	Shattered Dreams	4/2/88	6/4/88	1	14
	I Don't Want To Be A Hero	9/3/88	9/17/88	20	3

Artist	Title	Debut	Peak	Pos	Wks
Johnson, Don					
	Heartbeat	8/30/86	10/11/86	16	12
also see Streisand, Barbara & Don Johnson					
Joli, France					
	Come To Me	11/10/79	12/1/79	18	11
Jones, Howard					
	New Song	3/31/84	4/28/84	18	11
	Things Can Only Get Better	5/11/85	7/13/85	12	16
	Life In One Day	7/20/85	8/24/85	22	10
	No One Is To Blame	3/29/86	6/7/86	10	19
	You Know I Love You...Don't You	10/18/86	12/6/86	28	13
Jones, Oran "Juice"					
	The Rain	10/25/86	11/15/86	5	12
Journey					
	Lovin', Touchin', Squeezin'	9/22/79	11/10/79	2	25
	Any Way You Want It	4/5/80	5/10/80	17	18
	The Party's Over (Hopelessly In Love)	3/7/81	4/25/81	24	13
	Who's Crying Now	7/18/81	9/19/81	5	29
	Don't Stop Believin'	10/17/81	12/12/81	8	20
	Open Arms	1/16/82	3/13/82	4	23
	Still They Ride	5/22/82	7/3/82	22	13
	Separate Ways (Worlds Apart)	1/29/83	3/12/83	6	19
	Faithfully	4/23/83	6/11/83	19	18
	After The Fall	7/23/83	8/13/83	35	14
	Send Her My Love	10/22/83	11/19/83	36	9
	Only The Young	1/26/85	2/23/85	23	10
	Be Good To Yourself	4/12/86	5/17/86	21	11
	Suzanne	6/21/86	7/19/86	36	8
	Girl Can't Help It	8/30/86	10/4/86	42	9
	I'll Be Alright Without You	12/27/86	3/21/87	30	7
also see Bad English; Loggins, Kenny with Steve Perry and Steve Perry					
Judas Priest					
	You've Got Another Thing Comin'	10/16/82	11/20/82	20	13
Jump 'n the Saddle					
	The Curly Shuffle	11/12/83	12/17/83	1	19

Artist Title	Debut	Peak	Pos	Wks
Kajagoogoo				
Too Shy	6/18/83	7/23/83	8	14
also see Limahl				
Kansas				
Hold On	10/11/80	11/8/80	18	16
Got To Rock On	12/20/80	2/14/81	35	10
Play The Game Tonight	5/22/82	7/3/82	17	17
Fight Fire With Fire	9/17/83	10/22/83	26	8
All I Wanted	12/20/86	1/10/87	45	4
Katrina & the Waves				
Walking On Sunshine	5/18/85	6/15/85	11	13
KBC Band				
It's Not You, It's Not Me	11/29/86	12/20/86	47	4
also see Balin, Marty and Jefferson Starship				
KC & the Sunshine Band				
Please Don't Go	11/17/79	1/12/80	3	21
KC				
Give It Up	3/3/84	4/14/84	7	15
also see DeSario, Teri & KC				
Kemp, Johnny				
Just Got Paid	6/25/88	7/23/88	6	10
Kenny G				
Songbird	5/2/87	7/4/87	2	15
Khan, Chaka				
I Feel For You	9/29/84	12/8/84	1	23
Love Of A Lifetime	7/12/86	8/23/86	32	7
also see Rufus & Chaka Khan				
Kihn, Greg, Band				
The Breakup Song (They Don't Write 'Em)	7/25/81	9/26/81	10	19
Jeopardy	3/26/83	5/7/83	4	19
Kind				
Loved By You	8/14/82	10/2/82	15	20
I've Got You	4/14/84	4/21/84	31	6

Artist Title	Debut	Peak	Pos	Wks
King, Ben E.				
Stand By Me	11/1/86	12/27/86	2	15
King, Carole				
One Fine Day	7/5/80	8/9/80	18	11
Kings				
Switchin' To Glide	10/11/80	1/17/81	9	24
/This Beat Goes On	12/6/80	1/17/81	9	16
Kinks				
Come Dancing	5/28/83	7/30/83	5	18
Kiss				
Forever	3/31/90	5/5/90	11	6
Kix				
Don't Close Your Eyes	10/21/89	11/11/89	19	4
Klymaxx				
I Miss You	11/23/85	12/28/85	4	18
Man Size Love	7/5/86	8/30/86	14	14
I'd Still Say Yes	7/4/87	8/8/87	10	8
Knack				
My Sharona	7/28/79	8/18/79	1	27
Good Girls Don't	9/29/79	11/3/79	7	18
Baby Talks Dirty	2/9/80	3/15/80	11	13
Knight, Gladys & the Pips				
Landlord	7/5/80	7/26/80	34	8
also see (Warwick), Dionne & Friends				
Kon Kan				
I Beg Your Pardon	2/4/89	3/18/89	6	10
Kool & the Gang				
Ladies Night	10/27/79	12/1/79	8	25
Too Hot	2/16/80	3/29/80	11	16
Celebration	12/20/80	3/7/81	2	41
Take My Heart (You Can Have It If You Want It)	12/26/81	1/23/82	31	8
Get Down On It	5/1/82	6/19/82	14	19
Joanna	1/14/84	2/25/84	5	18
Tonight	4/7/84	5/19/84	13	15

Artist	Title	Debut	Peak	Pos	Wks
	Misled	3/2/85	3/30/85	14	12
	Fresh	5/4/85	6/1/85	12	12
	Cherish	8/10/85	10/5/85	1	20
	Emergency	11/2/85	12/14/85	26	13
	Victory	12/27/86	1/24/87	18	7
	Stone Love	4/4/87	5/2/87	15	6
Kool Moe Dee					
	Wild, Wild West	6/18/88	7/2/88	17	5
LaBelle, Patti					
	New Attitude	4/27/85	5/25/85	13	12
LaBelle, Patti & Michael McDonald					
	On My Own	4/26/86	5/31/86	1	18
also see McDonald, Michael					
Laid Back					
	White Horse	5/12/84	6/2/84	13	11
Lattisaw, Stacy					
	Love On A Two Way Street	8/8/81	9/12/81	19	11
Lauper, Cyndi					
	Girls Just Want To Have Fun	2/4/84	2/25/84	4	22
	Time After Time	5/5/84	6/2/84	3	17
	She Bop	8/25/84	9/29/84	2	17
	All Through The Night	10/27/84	12/15/84	11	15
	The Goonies 'R' Good Enough	5/18/85	6/15/85	23	14
	True Colors	8/30/86	11/1/86	6	17
	Change Of Heart	12/13/86	2/14/87	10	11
	What's Going On	3/21/87	4/25/87	19	8
also see the Hooters					
Lee, Johnny					
	Lookin' For Love	9/13/80	10/18/80	6	16
Lekakis, Paul					
	Boom Boom (Let's Go Back To My Room)	3/7/87	4/11/87	8	12
Lennon, John					
	(Just Like) Starting Over	11/15/80	12/27/80	1	26
	Woman	2/14/81	3/21/81	3	19
	Watching The Wheels	3/28/81	5/9/81	13	16

Artist	Title	Debut	Peak	Pos	Wks
	Nobody Told Me	1/28/84	2/18/84	11	13

also see the Beatles

Lennon, Julian

	Valotte	12/8/84	1/5/85	9	13
	Too Late For Goodbyes	1/26/85	3/23/85	9	17
	Say You're Wrong	5/4/85	5/25/85	25	9
	Stick Around	4/5/86	5/17/86	23	10

Lennox, Annie & Al Green

	Put A Little Love In Your Heart	12/31/88	1/21/89	21	4

also see Eurythmics

Level 42

	Something About You	3/29/86	6/14/86	8	19
	Lessons In Love	5/9/87	6/27/87	14	10

Levert

	Casanova	9/19/87	10/24/87	14	9

Lewis, Huey & the News

	Do You Believe In Love	3/6/82	5/8/82	11	20
	Workin' For A Livin'	8/14/82	10/9/82	34	11
	Heart And Soul	10/29/83	12/3/83	13	20
	I Want A New Drug	2/18/84	3/24/84	6	18
	The Heart Of Rock & Roll	5/26/84	6/30/84	8	16
	If This Is It	8/11/84	9/8/84	10	12
	Walking On A Thin Line	10/20/84	11/10/84	31	10
	The Power Of Love	6/29/85	8/3/85	2	19
	Back In Time	11/9/85	11/9/85	46	1
	Stuck With You	8/2/86	9/20/86	3	17
	Hip To Be Square	10/11/86	11/29/86	16	14
	Jacob's Ladder	12/20/86	3/14/87	7	15
	I Know What I Like	4/4/87	5/16/87	20	9
	Doing It All For My Baby	8/1/87	9/19/87	19	8
	Perfect World	7/30/88	8/27/88	15	5

Limahl

	Never Ending Story	6/1/85	7/13/85	17	10

also see Kajagoogoo

Artist Title	Debut	Peak	Pos	Wks
Linear				
Sending All My Love	4/28/90	5/5/90	22	2
Lipps, Inc.				
Funkytown	5/3/80	6/14/80	3	20
Lisa Lisa & Cult Jam with Full Force				
All Cried Out	10/11/86	11/15/86	4	14
Lisa Lisa & Cult Jam				
Head To Toe	4/11/87	6/20/87	2	16
Lost In Emotion	8/29/87	9/26/87	16	10
Little River Band				
Lonesome Loser	8/25/79	10/27/79	6	21
Cool Change	12/22/79	1/26/80	24	11
The Night Owls	10/3/81	11/14/81	5	20
Take It Easy On Me	2/20/82	3/27/82	19	16
The Other Guy	1/8/83	2/5/83	14	11
Living Colour				
Cult Of Personality	3/25/89	5/6/89	2	13
Living In A Box				
Living In A Box	7/4/87	8/15/87	29	7
L.L. Cool J				
I Need Love	8/15/87	9/19/87	14	7
I'm That Type Of Guy	6/10/89	7/15/89	5	7
Loggins, Kenny				
This Is It	1/19/80	3/15/80	6	23
I'm Alright	9/20/80	11/8/80	3	20
Heart To Heart	1/8/83	2/5/83	19	15
Welcome To Heartlight	3/19/83	5/7/83	18	15
Footloose	2/11/84	4/7/84	1	25
I'm Free (Heaven Helps The Man)	7/7/84	7/21/84	27	8
Vox Humana	3/23/85	4/27/85	26	10
Forever	7/6/85	8/3/85	31	11
Danger Zone	5/31/86	7/26/86	8	14
Meet Me Half Way	4/11/87	6/20/87	22	12
Nobody's Fool	7/30/88	8/20/88	21	5

Artist	Title	Debut	Peak	Pos	Wks
Loggins, Kenny with Steve Perry					
	Don't Fight It	8/28/82	10/16/82	5	18
also see Journey and Perry, Steve					
Lone Justice					
	Shelter	12/27/86	1/10/87	53	3
Lopez, Denise					
	If You Feel It	11/5/88	11/26/88	24	5
Lorain, A'me					
	Whole Wide World	4/14/90	5/5/90	15	4
Lorber, Jeff featuring Karyn White					
	Facts Of Love	1/24/87	2/28/87	20	6
also see White, Karyn					
Loring, Gloria & Carl Anderson					
	Friends And Lovers	8/9/86	9/20/86	1	16
Los Lobos					
	Set Me Free (Rosa Lee)	1/31/87	3/28/87	22	9
	La Bamba	7/11/87	9/5/87	1	21
	Come On, Let's Go	10/24/87	11/21/87	16	6
Love And Rockets					
	So Alive	6/17/89	7/29/89	3	15
Loverboy					
	Turn Me Loose	5/23/81	6/13/81	24	12
	Working For The Weekend	1/16/82	2/20/82	9	19
	When It's Over	4/17/82	6/12/82	21	17
	Hot Girls In Love	6/18/83	7/30/83	16	17
	Queen Of The Broken Hearts	10/15/83	11/5/83	29	8
	This Could Be The Night	2/8/86	4/5/86	23	12
	Heaven In Your Eyes	8/16/86	10/11/86	29	12
	Notorious	9/5/87	9/12/87	36	3
also see Reno, Mike & Ann Wilson					
Lowe, Nick & his Cowboy Outfit					
	I Knew The Bride (When She Use To Rock And Roll)	10/26/85	11/30/85	21	12
also see Carrack, Paul					

Artist	Title	Debut	Peak	Pos	Wks
M					
	Pop Muzik	9/29/79	12/22/79	3	23
Madhouse					
	Six	2/7/87	3/7/87	23	5
Madness					
	Our House	6/4/83	7/16/83	10	18
Madonna					
	Holiday	2/11/84	2/25/84	18	11
	Borderline	6/30/84	7/28/84	4	15
	Lucky Star	9/15/84	10/20/84	7	14
	Like A Virgin	11/24/84	1/5/85	1	19
	Material Girl	2/16/85	3/30/85	2	18
	Crazy For You	3/16/85	4/13/85	2	19
	Angel	4/27/85	6/15/85	7	15
	Into The Groove	6/8/85	7/6/85	3	15
	Dress You Up	8/17/85	9/28/85	7	15
	Live To Tell	4/19/86	6/14/86	2	16
	Papa Don't Preach	6/28/86	7/26/86	1	18
	True Blue	10/4/86	11/22/86	9	15
	Open Your Heart	12/13/86	2/14/87	3	14
	La Isla Bonita	3/7/87	5/16/87	3	17
	Who's That Girl	7/11/87	8/29/87	1	20
	Causing A Commotion	9/12/87	11/7/87	4	13
	Spotlight	12/12/87	1/30/88	15	9
	Like A Prayer	3/25/89	4/29/89	1	15
	Cherish	4/15/89	4/15/89	30	2
	Dear Jesse	4/15/89	5/27/89	16	7
	Express Yourself	5/27/89	6/24/89	12	6
	Cherish	8/26/89	9/9/89	18	5
Manchester, Melissa					
	You Should Hear How She Talks About You	8/7/82	10/2/82	3	18
Mancini, Henry					
	Ravel's Bolero	2/9/80	3/8/80	15	12
Mangione, Chuck					
	Give It All You Got	4/5/80	4/19/80	27	7

Artist Title	Debut	Peak	Pos	Wks
Manhattan Transfer				
Boy From New York City	7/4/81	8/8/81	10	18
Manhattans				
Shining Star	7/26/80	8/30/80	15	12
Manilow, Barry				
Ships	10/13/79	12/8/79	13	17
When I Wanted You	2/16/80	3/8/80	22	9
I Made It Through The Rain	11/29/80	1/10/81	20	15
The Old Songs	11/21/81	12/19/81	18	10
Read 'Em And Weep	12/24/83	1/14/84	30	10
Mann's, Manfred, Earth Band				
For You	4/18/81	5/30/81	14	18
Runner	2/25/84	4/14/84	16	14
Marie, Teena				
Lovergirl	3/2/85	4/6/85	10	13
M/A/R/R/S				
Pump Up The Volume	1/2/88	2/13/88	1	17
Martika				
More Than You Know	3/11/89	4/1/89	18	5
Toy Soldiers	6/17/89	8/5/89	1	16
I Feel The Earth Move	9/23/89	10/21/89	12	5
Martin, Marilyn				
Night Moves	2/8/86	3/29/86	42	8
also see Collins, Phil & Marilyn Martin				
Martinez, Nancy				
For Tonight	12/13/86	1/24/87	17	8
Marx, Richard				
Don't Mean Nothing	5/30/87	8/29/87	6	19
Should've Known Better	9/26/87	12/5/87	4	13
Endless Summer Nights	1/23/88	4/2/88	1	15
Hold On To The Nights	5/21/88	7/30/88	3	15
Satisfied	5/6/89	6/24/89	8	11
Right Here Waiting	7/8/89	8/26/89	1	16
Angelia	10/7/89	12/2/89	3	15

Artist	Title	Debut	Peak	Pos	Wks
	Too Late To Say Goodbye	2/3/90	3/10/90	9	7
	Children Of The Night	5/5/90	5/5/90	28	1
Mary Jane Girls					
	In My House	5/4/85	6/15/85	10	14
	Walk Like A Man	7/12/86	8/9/86	23	8
M.C. Hammer					
	U Can't Touch This	4/14/90	5/5/90	6	4
McCartney, Paul & Wings					
	Coming Up (Live At Glasgow)	4/26/80	6/28/80	1	24
McCartney, Paul with Stevie Wonder					
	Ebony And Ivory	4/17/82	5/22/82	1	22
McCartney, Paul					
	Take It Away	7/24/82	9/4/82	13	15
	No More Lonely Nights	10/13/84	11/24/84	10	16
	Spies Like Us	11/30/85	2/1/86	7	16
	Press	8/16/86	9/20/86	14	9
McCartney, Paul & Michael Jackson					
	Say Say Say	10/15/83	12/10/83	2	24

also see the Beatles; Jackson, Michael and Wonder, Stevie

McClinton, Delbert					
	Giving It Up For Your Love	2/14/81	3/14/81	23	9
McDonald, Michael					
	I Keep Forgettin' (Every Time You're Near)	8/28/82	10/16/82	7	17
	I Gotta Try	1/15/83	1/29/83	40	4
	No Lookin' Back	8/10/85	9/14/85	36	7
	Sweet Freedom	6/14/86	8/30/86	11	17

also see the Doobie Brothers; Ingram, James and LaBelle, Patti

McFerrin, Bobby					
	Don't Worry Be Happy	8/20/88	9/24/88	1	13
McKenzie, Bob & Doug					
	Take Off	2/13/82	3/13/82	5	14

also see Rush

McLean, Don					
	Crying	3/7/81	4/4/81	15	12

Artist Title	Debut	Peak	Pos	Wks
McVie, Christine				
Got A Hold On Me	2/18/84	3/24/84	21	14
also see Fleetwood Mac				
Meco				
Ewok Celebration	7/9/83	8/20/83	4	15
Medeiros, Glenn				
Nothing's Gonna Change My Love For You	2/28/87	5/23/87	4	20
Medley, Bill & Jennifer Warnes				
(I've Had) The Time Of My Life	10/10/87	12/5/87	2	17
also see Cocker, Joe & Jennifer Warnes				
Meisner, Randy				
Hearts On Fire	1/17/81	3/21/81	15	16
also see the Eagles and Poco				
Men At Work				
Who Can It Be Now	8/14/82	10/30/82	2	27
Down Under	12/11/82	2/5/83	2	22
Overkill	4/23/83	5/21/83	6	17
It's A Mistake	7/9/83	8/6/83	17	14
Men Without Hats				
The Safety Dance	8/27/83	9/24/83	1	20
Pop Goes The World	12/26/87	2/13/88	9	9
Mendes, Sergio				
Never Gonna Let You Go	6/11/83	8/20/83	2	20
Alibis	7/28/84	8/25/84	13	10
Metallica				
One	5/13/89	5/27/89	13	5
Miami Sound Machine				
Conga	1/18/86	3/1/86	3	14
Bad Boy	3/15/86	4/26/86	16	15
Words Get In The Way	8/9/86	10/11/86	4	16
Falling In Love (Uh-Oh)	11/29/86	1/17/87	21	9
Gloria Estefan & Miami Sound Machine				
Rhythm Is Gonna Get You	6/13/87	7/25/87	6	10
Anything For You	4/16/88	5/21/88	5	10

Artist Title	Debut	Peak	Pos	Wks
1-2-3	7/2/88	8/6/88	3	11

also see Estefan, Gloria

Michael, George
I Want Your Sex	5/30/87	8/1/87	1	23
Faith	10/31/87	12/19/87	1	17
Father Figure	2/6/88	3/12/88	2	13
One More Try	4/30/88	6/11/88	1	16
Monkey	7/9/88	9/3/88	1	13

also see Estus, Deon with George Michael and Wham!

Midler, Bette
The Rose	5/17/80	6/28/80	2	23
Wind Beneath My Wings	5/13/89	6/10/89	1	15

Mike + the Mechanics
Silent Running (On Dangerous Ground)	11/16/85	3/1/86	14	22
All I Need Is A Miracle	3/22/86	5/24/86	13	16
Taken In	7/19/86	8/30/86	38	10
The Living Years	2/11/89	3/25/89	1	14

also see Carrack, Paul; Genesis and Young, Paul

Miller, Steve, Band
Abracadabra	6/19/82	8/28/82	2	25

also see Scaggs, Boz

Milli Vanilli
Girl You Know It's True	2/25/89	4/22/89	1	12
Baby Don't Forget My Number	5/13/89	7/1/89	1	16
Girl I'm Gonna Miss You	8/19/89	9/16/89	1	15
Blame It On The Rain	10/28/89	11/25/89	2	17
All Or Nothing	1/13/90	2/24/90	5	13

Mills, Stephanie
Never Knew Love Like This Before	11/1/80	11/29/80	11	16

Milsap, Ronnie
(There's) No Gettin' Over Me	9/12/81	10/17/81	19	12

Ministry
Everyday Is Halloween	3/4/89	4/22/89	15	10

Artist	Title	Debut	Peak	Pos	Wks
Minogue, Kylie					
	I Should Be So Lucky	7/2/88	7/16/88	21	5
	The Loco-Motion	8/20/88	10/22/88	3	15
Models					
	Out Of Mind Out Of Sight	5/10/86	6/28/86	25	10
Mondo Rock					
	Primitive Love Rites	5/16/87	6/6/87	37	4
Money, Eddie					
	Think I'm In Love	7/3/82	8/28/82	15	21
	Take Me Home Tonight	9/20/86	11/29/86	6	17
	I Wanna Go Back	1/10/87	2/7/87	30	5
	Walk On Water	10/15/88	11/19/88	17	7
	Peace In Our Time	12/9/89	2/3/90	9	14
Monkees					
	That Was Then, This Is Now	7/5/86	8/30/86	17	13
Moody Blues					
	Gemini Dream	6/27/81	8/8/81	11	15
	The Voice	8/8/81	9/19/81	11	15
	Sitting At The Wheel	10/1/83	10/22/83	25	8
	Your Wildest Dreams	4/26/86	6/21/86	16	17
	The Other Side Of Life	8/23/86	9/27/86	46	6
Morales, Michael					
	Who Do You Give Your Love To	5/20/89	6/17/89	22	8
	What I Like About You	8/5/89	8/26/89	22	4
Motels					
	Only The Lonely	5/8/82	8/14/82	7	23
	Suddenly Last Summer	10/22/83	11/19/83	15	13
Motley Crue					
	Looks That Kill	2/25/84	3/31/84	14	13
	Smokin' In The Boys Room	8/17/85	9/14/85	10	11
	Girls, Girls, Girls	5/23/87	7/25/87	9	13
	Dr. Feelgood	9/2/89	10/21/89	2	9
	Without You	3/3/90	4/21/90	8	10
Moving Pictures					
	What About Me	1/29/83	2/26/83	11	17

Artist Title	Debut	Peak	Pos	Wks
Mr. Mister				
Broken Wings	10/5/85	12/14/85	3	20
Kyrie	12/21/85	3/15/86	2	19
Is It Love	3/29/86	5/31/86	26	13
Murphy, Eddie				
Party All The Time	11/16/85	12/21/85	3	18
Murray, Anne				
Broken Hearted Me	11/17/79	12/15/79	24	10
Musical Youth				
Pass The Dutchie	2/5/83	2/26/83	8	13
Myles, Alannah				
Black Velvet	2/24/90	3/31/90	1	11
Naked Eyes				
Always Something There To Remind Me	5/28/83	7/9/83	5	15
Promises, Promises	8/20/83	10/22/83	7	18
also see Climie Fisher				
Nash, Graham				
Innocent Eyes	5/10/86	6/21/86	41	7
also see Crosby, Stills & Nash				
Nelson, Willie				
Always On My Mind	6/5/82	7/3/82	6	22
also see Iglesias, Julio & Willie Nelson				
Nena				
99 Red Balloons	1/28/84	2/25/84	1	17
/99 Luftballons	1/28/84	2/25/84	1	6
Nevil, Robbie				
C'est La Vie	11/8/86	1/24/87	3	17
Wot's It To Ya	5/30/87	7/18/87	28	8
New Edition				
Cool It Now	11/3/84	12/22/84	1	20
Mr. Telephone Man	1/26/85	3/2/85	6	10
If It Isn't Love	8/20/88	9/24/88	6	9
also see Bell Biv DeVoe and Brown, Bobby				

Artist Title	Debut	Peak	Pos	Wks
New Kids On The Block				
Please Don't Go Girl	9/3/88	10/8/88	11	7
You Got It (The Right Stuff)	12/17/88	2/11/89	11	12
I'll Be Loving You (Forever)	4/15/89	6/10/89	7	15
Hangin' Tough	7/15/89	8/19/89	1	13
/Didn't I (Blow Your Mind)	9/23/89	11/11/89	4	10
Cover Girl	9/16/89	11/11/89	2	14
This One's For The Children	11/18/89	1/6/90	3	14
New Order				
Bizarre Love Triangle	2/28/87	4/4/87	13	7
True Faith	12/12/87	1/16/88	13	7
Newton, Juice				
Angel Of The Morning	4/4/81	5/30/81	5	21
Queen Of Hearts	7/11/81	10/10/81	4	27
The Sweetest Thing (I've Ever Known)	1/16/82	2/20/82	15	11
Love's Been A Little Bit Hard On Me	6/19/82	8/14/82	16	18
Newton-John, Olivia				
Magic	7/5/80	8/23/80	1	23
Physical	10/24/81	12/5/81	1	30
Make A Move On Me	4/3/82	5/8/82	12	13
Heart Attack	10/9/82	11/6/82	4	17
Twist Of Fate	12/17/83	1/21/84	14	15
Soul Kiss	10/5/85	11/9/85	15	12
Newton-John, Olivia & Electric Light Orchestra				
Xanadu	9/20/80	10/25/80	10	13

also see Electric Light Orchestra and Gibb, Andy & Olivia Newton-John

Artist Title	Debut	Peak	Pos	Wks
Nicks, Stevie with Tom Petty & the Heartbreakers				
Stop Draggin' My Heart Around	8/1/81	9/26/81	7	21
Nicks, Stevie with Don Henley				
Leather And Lace	10/31/81	12/12/81	11	19
Nicks, Stevie				
Edge Of Seventeen (Just Like The White Winged Dove)	1/30/82	3/27/82	11	17
Stand Back	6/18/83	8/20/83	12	19
If Anyone Falls	10/15/83	11/12/83	20	13
Talk To Me	11/16/85	1/11/86	15	17

Artist	Title	Debut	Peak	Pos	Wks
	I Can't Wait	2/22/86	3/22/86	30	8

also see Fleetwood Mac; Henley, Don and Petty, Tom

Night Ranger

	Title	Debut	Peak	Pos	Wks
	Don't Tell Me You Love Me	2/12/83	3/26/83	16	15
	Sing Me Away	4/23/83	5/28/83	40	9
	Sister Christian	5/12/84	6/23/84	2	15
	When You Close Your Eyes	8/11/84	9/22/84	9	13
	Sentimental Street	6/8/85	8/10/85	14	15
	Four In The Morning (I Can't Take Any More)	9/21/85	10/19/85	17	9
	Goodbye	11/30/85	1/25/86	16	14

Nova, Aldo

	Title	Debut	Peak	Pos	Wks
	Fantasy	3/27/82	5/8/82	16	18

Nu Shooz

	Title	Debut	Peak	Pos	Wks
	I Can't Wait	4/26/86	6/7/86	4	15

Numan, Gary

	Title	Debut	Peak	Pos	Wks
	Cars	4/19/80	5/31/80	5	20

Nylons

	Title	Debut	Peak	Pos	Wks
	Kiss Him Goodbye	5/16/87	7/25/87	11	12

Oak Ridge Boys

	Title	Debut	Peak	Pos	Wks
	Elvira	6/6/81	7/11/81	7	34
	Bobbie Sue	4/3/82	4/24/82	21	11

O'Banion, John

	Title	Debut	Peak	Pos	Wks
	Love You Like I Never Loved Before	5/16/81	6/6/81	38	6

Ocasek, Ric

	Title	Debut	Peak	Pos	Wks
	Emotion In Motion	9/13/86	11/15/86	25	14
	True To You	12/27/86	2/7/87	29	7

also see the Cars

Ocean, Billy

	Title	Debut	Peak	Pos	Wks
	Caribbean Queen (No More Love On The Run)	9/29/84	11/24/84	3	19
	Loverboy	1/12/85	2/16/85	4	15
	Suddenly	5/11/85	6/15/85	5	13
	Mystery Lady	8/3/85	8/31/85	26	8
	When The Going Gets Tough, The Tough Get Going	12/14/85	2/8/86	3	19
	There'll Be Sad Songs (To Make You Cry)	4/26/86	7/12/86	10	18

Artist	Title	Debut	Peak	Pos	Wks
	Love Zone	9/6/86	10/11/86	18	8
	Get Outta My Dreams, Get Into My Car	3/12/88	4/16/88	1	16
O'Connor, Sinead					
	Nothing Compares 2 U	3/24/90	4/28/90	1	7
Off Broadway					
	Stay In Time	3/29/80	5/10/80	9	19
Ollie & Jerry					
	Breakin'...There's No Stopping Us	7/21/84	8/11/84	10	10
also see Parker Jr., Ray & Raydio					
Ono, Yoko					
	Walking On Thin Ice	3/7/81	3/21/81	23	10
Orchestral Manoeuvres In The Dark					
	So In Love	10/5/85	11/23/85	21	11
	If You Leave	3/29/86	5/24/86	9	15
	(Forever) Live And Die	11/1/86	12/6/86	26	9
	Dreaming	5/14/88	5/28/88	19	5
Orr, Benjamin					
	Stay The Night	12/13/86	1/10/87	37	5
also see the Cars					
Osborne, Jeffrey					
	On The Wings Of Love	1/8/83	1/29/83	26	9
	You Should Be Mine (The Woo Woo Song)	7/5/86	8/16/86	24	11
also see Warwick, Dionne & Jeffrey Osborne					
Osbourne, Ozzy					
	Crazy Train	8/8/81	9/5/81	19	11
Osmond, Donny					
	Soldier Of Love	3/25/89	6/3/89	3	13
	Sacred Emotion	7/8/89	8/5/89	20	6
Other Ones					
	Holiday	7/25/87	9/12/87	18	10
Outfield					
	Your Love	3/15/86	5/24/86	6	16
	All The Love In The World	6/28/86	8/23/86	33	11
	Everytime You Cry	10/11/86	11/1/86	47	4

Artist	Title	Debut	Peak	Pos	Wks
	Since You've Been Gone	7/11/87	8/22/87	15	9
	No Surrender	9/26/87	10/10/87	34	4
Paige, Kevin					
	Don't Shut Me Out	11/18/89	12/9/89	23	5
Palmer, Robert					
	Addicted To Love	3/1/86	5/10/86	1	18
	I Didn't Mean To Turn You On	8/16/86	11/8/86	3	19
	Simply Irresistible	7/9/88	9/17/88	1	13
	Early In The Morning	12/3/88	12/24/88	21	4
	Purple Haze	1/21/89	2/18/89	15	6
also see the Power Station					
Parker, Jr., Ray					
	The Other Woman	5/15/82	6/19/82	3	18
	Bad Boy	2/5/83	2/26/83	23	8
	I Still Can't Get Over Loving You	1/7/84	2/11/84	13	18
	Ghostbusters	7/7/84	8/4/84	1	23
	Jamie	12/22/84	1/26/85	22	11
Parker, Jr., Ray & Raydio					
	Two Places At The Same Time	6/21/80	7/5/80	33	5
	A Woman Needs Love (Just Like You Do)	5/30/81	6/27/81	12	14
also see Ollie & Jerry					
Parr, John					
	Naughty Naughty	2/16/85	3/23/85	30	8
	St. Elmo's Fire (Man In Motion)	7/6/85	8/24/85	1	20
Parsons, Alan, Project					
	Games People Play	1/17/81	2/28/81	8	19
	Time	6/27/81	8/1/81	16	16
	Eye In The Sky	9/18/82	10/30/82	3	18
	Don't Answer Me	4/7/84	5/5/84	21	11
Parton, Dolly					
	9 To 5	1/17/81	3/7/81	1	25
also see Rogers, Kenny with Dolly Parton					
Pebbles					
	Girlfriend	2/27/88	4/23/88	4	11
	Mercedes Boy	6/4/88	7/30/88	2	13

Artist	Title	Debut	Peak	Pos	Wks
Penn, Michael					
	No Myth	3/3/90	3/31/90	10	8
Perfect Gentlemen					
	Ooh La La (I Can't Get Over You)	4/14/90	5/5/90	20	4
Perry, Steve					
	Oh Sherrie	4/14/84	5/12/84	7	17
	Foolish Heart	12/8/84	1/26/85	33	14
also see Journey and Loggins, Kenny with Steve Perry					
Pet Shop Boys					
	West End Girls	3/8/86	5/17/86	1	18
	Opportunities (Let's Make Lots Of Money)	6/14/86	8/2/86	25	11
	It's A Sin	9/5/87	10/31/87	5	13
	Always On My Mind	4/9/88	5/14/88	4	9
Pet Shop Boys & Dusty Springfield					
	What Have I Done To Deserve This	12/26/87	2/20/88	4	15
Petty, Tom & the Heartbreakers					
	Don't Do Me Like That	12/22/79	2/9/80	6	21
	Refugee	3/15/80	4/12/80	13	17
	The Waiting	5/9/81	6/20/81	12	19
	You Got Lucky	11/27/82	1/8/83	20	15
	Change Of Heart	3/19/83	4/16/83	19	11
	Don't Come Around Here No More	4/6/85	5/11/85	12	12
	Jammin' Me	4/18/87	6/13/87	21	11
Petty, Tom & the Heartbreakers with Stevie Nicks					
	Needles And Pins	2/1/86	3/1/86	22	8
Petty, Tom					
	Runnin' Down A Dream	8/12/89	9/9/89	12	7
	Free Fallin'	12/30/89	1/27/90	2	19
also see Nicks, Stevie and the Traveling Wilburys					
Pink Floyd					
	Another Brick In The Wall (Part II)	2/9/80	3/22/80	1	27
	Not Now John	6/4/83	6/18/83	31	8
Plant, Robert					
	Burning Down One Side	9/18/82	10/16/82	23	10
	Big Log	8/20/83	10/1/83	20	18
	Little By Little	6/29/85	7/13/85	25	6

Artist	Title	Debut	Peak	Pos	Wks
	Tall Cool One	5/14/88	6/18/88	12	7

also see the Honeydrippers

Poco
	Call It Love	9/2/89	10/28/89	11	10

also see Meisner, Randy and Schmit, Timothy B.

Point Blank
	Nicole	8/15/81	10/10/81	9	18

Pointer Sisters
	He's So Shy	10/25/80	12/13/80	5	18
	Slow Hand	7/25/81	8/29/81	7	18
	Should I Do It	3/6/82	4/17/82	30	13
	American Music	8/14/82	9/11/82	24	9
	Automatic	2/25/84	5/5/84	7	18
	Jump (For My Love)	5/19/84	7/14/84	7	18
	I'm So Excited	9/8/84	10/20/84	2	20
	Neutron Dance	1/19/85	2/23/85	7	15
	Dare Me	7/27/85	9/21/85	20	16

Poison
	Talk Dirty To Me	3/21/87	5/16/87	7	13
	I Want Action	6/6/87	7/18/87	23	9
	I Won't Forget You	9/5/87	9/5/87	43	1
	Rock And Roll All Nite	12/19/87	2/13/88	11	10
	Nothin' But A Good Time	4/16/88	6/4/88	6	11
	Fallen Angel	8/27/88	10/8/88	8	9
	Every Rose Has Its Thorn	10/29/88	12/24/88	1	18
	Your Mama Don't Dance	2/18/89	4/8/89	6	10

Police
	De Do Do Do, De Da Da Da	12/6/80	1/24/81	7	20
	Don't Stand So Close To Me	2/21/81	4/4/81	8	19
	Every Little Thing She Does Is Magic	10/17/81	12/12/81	6	24
	Every Breath You Take	6/4/83	8/6/83	1	28
	King Of Pain	9/3/83	10/15/83	9	18
	Synchronicity II	11/5/83	12/3/83	18	15
	Wrapped Around Your Finger	1/14/84	2/18/84	18	15
	Don't Stand So Close To Me '86	10/25/86	12/6/86	19	9

also see Sting

Artist Title	Debut	Peak	Pos	Wks

Power Station
Some Like It Hot	3/16/85	5/4/85	10	17
Get It On (Bang A Gong)	6/8/85	7/27/85	17	15

also see Duran Duran and Palmer, Robert

Preston, Billy & Syreeta
With You I'm Born Again	2/2/80	4/12/80	7	23

Pretenders
Brass In Pocket (I'm Special)	4/12/80	5/24/80	4	22
Back On The Chain Gang	1/22/83	2/26/83	7	19
Middle Of The Road	2/4/84	2/25/84	14	13
Show Me	4/28/84	5/12/84	29	7
Don't Get Me Wrong	10/11/86	11/22/86	21	14
My Baby	2/21/87	3/14/87	24	4

also see UB40 with Chrissie Hynde

Pretty Poison
Catch Me (I'm Falling)	11/7/87	12/12/87	4	15

Priest, Maxi
Wild World	11/5/88	12/10/88	15	7

Prince
I Wanna Be Your Lover	2/9/80	3/1/80	21	8
Little Red Corvette	5/14/83	6/25/83	4	18
1999	7/9/83	9/10/83	6	20
Delirious	10/15/83	11/12/83	10	15
When Doves Cry	6/16/84	7/7/84	1	21
Let's Go Crazy	8/25/84	9/22/84	3	25
Purple Rain	10/6/84	11/3/84	2	18
Darling Nikki	11/3/84	11/24/84	46	5
I Would Die 4 U	12/8/84	1/19/85	5	15
Take Me With U	3/9/85	3/23/85	31	6
Raspberry Beret	5/18/85	7/20/85	4	17
Pop Life	7/27/85	8/31/85	11	12
Kiss	2/22/86	4/19/86	1	18
Mountains	5/24/86	6/28/86	15	10
Sign 'O' The Times	4/11/87	5/2/87	17	5
U Got The Look	7/25/87	10/17/87	1	20
I Could Never Take The Place Of Your Man	11/21/87	1/23/88	10	11

Artist	Title	Debut	Peak	Pos	Wks
	Alphabet St.	6/11/88	7/2/88	11	5
	When 2 R In Love	8/6/88	8/20/88	22	4
Prism					
	Don't Let Him Know	1/30/82	3/20/82	22	15
Pseudo Echo					
	Funky Town	5/9/87	7/18/87	3	17
Psychedelic Furs					
	Heartbreak Beat	4/4/87	5/23/87	11	9
Pure Prairie League					
	Let Me Love You Tonight	6/21/80	7/19/80	20	13
Q-Feel					
	Dancing In Heaven (Orbital Be-Bop)	6/24/89	7/22/89	16	7
Quarterflash					
	Harden My Heart	12/12/81	2/6/82	3	21
	Find Another Fool	3/20/82	4/24/82	17	11
	Take Me To Heart	7/23/83	8/20/83	22	14
Queen					
	Crazy Little Thing Called Love	1/26/80	3/8/80	1	22
	Another One Bites The Dust	9/6/80	9/27/80	1	30
	Body Language	5/15/82	6/19/82	9	16
	Radio Ga-Ga	3/24/84	4/14/84	19	10
	A Kind Of Magic	6/21/86	7/12/86	37	6
Queen & David Bowie					
	Under Pressure	11/28/81	1/23/82	7	15
also see Bowie, David					
Quiet Riot					
	Cum On Feel The Noize	9/17/83	10/29/83	3	22
Rabbitt, Eddie					
	Drivin' My Life Away	9/13/80	10/18/80	5	24
	I Love A Rainy Night	1/17/81	3/7/81	4	19
	Step By Step	9/19/81	10/31/81	8	15
Rabbitt, Eddie with Crystal Gayle					
	You And I	1/15/83	2/12/83	11	21
also see Gayle, Crystal					

Artist	Title	Debut	Peak	Pos	Wks
Ratt					
	Round And Round	7/28/84	8/25/84	8	13
	Dance	3/21/87	4/18/87	23	5
Ray, Goodman & Brown					
	Special Lady	2/23/80	4/5/80	8	19
Ready For The World					
	Oh Sheila	9/7/85	10/12/85	1	16
	Love You Down	1/10/87	2/28/87	2	11
Real Life					
	Send Me An Angel	5/27/89	7/8/89	8	8
Regina					
	Baby Love	8/9/86	9/27/86	9	13
R.E.M.					
	Superman	11/29/86	12/27/86	24	7
	The One I Love	10/31/87	12/5/87	7	9
	Stand	1/28/89	3/4/89	3	10
Reno, Mike & Ann Wilson					
	Almost Paradise... Love Theme From Footloose	6/9/84	7/7/84	12	12

also see Heart; Loverboy and Wilson, Ann & Robin Zander

Artist	Title	Debut	Peak	Pos	Wks
REO Speedwagon					
	Keep On Loving You	11/22/80	2/7/81	1	30
	Take It On The Run	3/21/81	5/16/81	5	21
	Don't Let Him Go	6/13/81	7/25/81	25	12
	Keep The Fire Burnin'	6/12/82	8/7/82	13	17
	Sweet Time	10/2/82	10/23/82	20	9
	I Do'wanna Know	10/20/84	12/1/84	35	10
	Can't Fight This Feeling	1/19/85	3/16/85	3	19
	One Lonely Night	3/30/85	4/27/85	38	11
	Live Every Moment	7/20/85	8/10/85	46	8
	In My Dreams	9/19/87	10/31/87	17	9
Replacements					
	I'll Be You	4/15/89	5/6/89	15	5
Richard, Cliff					
	We Don't Talk Anymore	12/8/79	2/9/80	4	17

Artist	Title	Debut	Peak	Pos	Wks
	Dreaming	10/25/80	12/6/80	17	19
	A Little In Love	2/21/81	3/21/81	21	12

Richie, Lionel

	Truly	11/6/82	12/4/82	1	28
	You Are	2/19/83	4/9/83	5	19
	My Love	5/28/83	6/25/83	20	10
	All Night Long (All Night)	10/15/83	11/26/83	1	24
	Running With The Night	1/7/84	2/4/84	14	16
	Hello	3/24/84	5/5/84	1	22
	Stuck On You	7/21/84	8/18/84	5	14
	Penny Lover	10/6/84	11/10/84	18	16
	Say You, Say Me	11/2/85	12/28/85	1	21
	Dancing On The Ceiling	7/19/86	9/13/86	4	17
	Love Will Conquer All	10/4/86	12/13/86	17	15
	Deep River Woman *(with Alabama)*	12/13/86	2/21/87	3	14
	/Ballerina Girl	1/17/87	2/21/87	3	9
	Se La	3/28/87	5/2/87	20	6

also see the Commodores and Ross, Diana & Lionel Richie

Rob Base & D.J. E-Z Rock

	Joy And Pain	8/19/89	9/23/89	9	10

Robinson, Smokey

	Cruisin'	1/26/80	3/1/80	14	14
	Let Me Be The Clock	5/10/80	5/24/80	30	8
	Being With You	4/25/81	6/6/81	7	15
	Just To See Her	4/18/87	6/13/87	12	11
	One Heartbeat	9/5/87	10/3/87	12	8

Rockwell

	Somebody's Watching Me	2/18/84	3/24/84	1	16
	Obscene Phone Caller	7/14/84	7/28/84	25	6

Roger

	I Want To Be Your Man	12/12/87	2/13/88	3	13

Rogers, Kenny

	You Decorated My Life	10/20/79	11/17/79	14	16
	Coward Of The County	12/15/79	1/26/80	2	22
	Love The World Away	7/19/80	8/16/80	14	12
	Lady	10/18/80	12/6/80	1	25

Artist	Title	Debut	Peak	Pos	Wks
	I Don't Need You	7/4/81	8/15/81	7	17
	Share Your Love With Me	10/17/81	11/7/81	34	8
	Through The Years	3/6/82	3/27/82	21	12
	Love Will Turn You Around	9/4/82	10/2/82	21	11

Rogers, Kenny with Kim Carnes

	Don't Fall In Love With A Dreamer	4/19/80	5/31/80	7	19

Rogers, Kenny & Sheena Easton

	We've Got Tonight	2/19/83	3/26/83	10	19

Rogers, Kenny with Dolly Parton

	Islands In The Stream	9/24/83	11/12/83	1	22

Rogers, Kenny with Kim Carnes & James Ingram

	What About Me	11/10/84	12/1/84	14	10

also see Carnes, Kim; Easton, Sheena; Ingram, James and Parton, Dolly

Rolling Stones

	Emotional Rescue	7/12/80	8/23/80	3	19
	She's So Cold	11/29/80	12/13/80	35	7
	Start Me Up	8/22/81	10/3/81	2	30
	Waiting On A Friend	12/12/81	1/23/82	13	14
	Going To A Go-Go	6/12/82	7/24/82	14	16
	Undercover Of The Night	11/12/83	12/24/83	7	14
	Harlem Shuffle	3/15/86	4/12/86	5	13
	Mixed Emotions	9/2/89	9/30/89	6	6
	Almost Hear You Sigh	3/17/90	3/31/90	21	4

also see Jagger, Mick

Romantics

	Talking In Your Sleep	12/17/83	1/28/84	4	17

Ronstadt, Linda

	How Do I Make You	3/15/80	4/19/80	16	14
	Hurt So Bad	5/3/80	5/31/80	13	14
	I Can't Let Go	7/26/80	9/13/80	31	10
	Get Closer	10/30/82	11/20/82	22	11

Ronstadt, Linda & James Ingram

	Somewhere Out There	1/24/87	3/21/87	3	13

Ronstadt, Linda featuring Aaron Neville

	Don't Know Much	11/11/89	12/16/89	4	16

also see Ingram, James with Michael McDonald

Artist	Title	Debut	Peak	Pos	Wks
Ross, Diana					
	Upside Down	8/9/80	10/4/80	2	25
	It's My Turn	12/27/80	1/31/81	23	12
	Why Do Fools Fall In Love	12/26/81	1/16/82	19	11
	Muscles	12/11/82	1/8/83	26	9
	Swept Away	10/27/84	11/10/84	23	8
	Missing You	3/9/85	4/13/85	5	14
Ross, Diana & Lionel Richie					
	Endless Love	8/8/81	9/5/81	1	27

also see the Commodores; Iglesias, Julio & Diana Ross and Richie, Lionel

Roth, David Lee					
	California Girls	1/19/85	2/23/85	5	16
	Just A Gigolo/I Ain't Got Nobody	4/27/85	5/25/85	12	12
	Yankee Rose	8/2/86	8/23/86	15	10
	That's Life	11/15/86	11/22/86	49	4
	Just Like Paradise	1/23/88	3/5/88	5	10

also see Van Halen

Roxanne					
	Play That Funky Music	2/13/88	4/9/88	17	9
Roxette					
	The Look	2/18/89	4/8/89	4	12
	Dressed For Success	6/24/89	7/22/89	9	7
	Listen To Your Heart	10/28/89	11/4/89	17	6
	Dangerous	1/20/90	3/17/90	2	16
Roxy Music					
	Love Is The Drug	8/19/89	9/2/89	21	5

also see Carrack, Paul

Royal Philharmonic Orchestra					
	Hooked On Classics	1/9/82	2/20/82	12	18
Rufus & Chaka Khan					
	Do You Love What You Feel	1/19/80	2/16/80	26	9
	Ain't Nobody	12/24/83	1/28/84	18	15

also see Khan, Chaka

Artist	Title	Debut	Peak	Pos	Wks
Run-D.M.C.					
	Walk This Way	8/9/86	9/27/86	4	15
	You Be Illin'	12/13/86	1/24/87	13	8
Rush					
	The Spirit Of Radio	3/29/80	4/26/80	16	12
	Tom Sawyer	5/23/81	6/27/81	5	19
	Closer To The Heart	11/21/81	12/19/81	20	12
	New World Man	9/25/82	10/16/82	15	14
	The Big Money	11/16/85	12/21/85	39	6
	also see McKenzie, Bob & Doug				
Rushen, Patrice					
	Forget Me Nots	6/19/82	8/7/82	11	14
Sade					
	Smooth Operator	4/20/85	6/8/85	7	13
	The Sweetest Taboo	1/11/86	2/22/86	9	14
	Never As Good As The First Time	4/19/86	5/17/86	33	7
Sa-Fire					
	Boy, I've Been Told	10/29/88	11/26/88	10	8
	Thinking Of You	4/29/89	5/20/89	15	6
Saga					
	On The Loose	1/15/83	2/5/83	25	14
	Wind Him Up	4/16/83	5/7/83	30	8
Salt-N-Pepa					
	Push It	1/30/88	3/5/88	2	12
	Shake Your Thang	10/15/88	12/10/88	10	10
Santana					
	Winning	5/30/81	8/1/81	3	21
	Searchin'	9/5/81	10/3/81	34	8
	Hold On	10/2/82	10/16/82	17	11
Saraya					
	Timeless Love	12/16/89	1/20/90	14	6
Sayer, Leo					
	More Than I Can Say	11/8/80	12/27/80	8	20
	Living In A Fantasy	1/24/81	3/21/81	32	13

Artist	Title	Debut	Peak	Pos	Wks
Scaggs, Boz					
	Breakdown Dead Ahead	5/17/80	6/7/80	25	10
	Look What You've Done To Me	10/4/80	11/15/80	9	13
also see Miller, Steve, Band					
Scandal					
	Love's Got A Line On You	5/14/83	6/11/83	20	13
Scandal featuring Patty Smyth					
	The Warrior	8/11/84	9/29/84	11	15
Scarbury, Joey					
	Theme From "Greatest American Hero" (Believe It Or Not)	6/27/81	8/22/81	2	24
Schilling, Peter					
	Major Tom (Coming Home)	12/3/83	1/7/84	6	14
Schmit, Timothy B.					
	Boys Night Out	9/26/87	11/7/87	27	8
also see the Eagles and Poco					
Scorpions					
	No One Like You	5/15/82	7/10/82	26	24
	Rock You Like A Hurricane	3/31/84	5/5/84	12	16
	Rhythm Of Love	4/23/88	6/11/88	15	9
Scritti Politti					
	Perfect Way	10/19/85	12/21/85	18	17
Seduction					
	Two To Make It Right	12/30/89	2/10/90	7	13
Seger, Bob					
	Fire Lake	3/22/80	5/3/80	6	21
	Against The Wind	5/31/80	7/12/80	4	17
	You'll Accomp'ny Me	8/30/80	10/4/80	14	13
	Tryin' To Live My Life Without You	9/12/81	10/24/81	4	22
	Shame On The Moon	12/18/82	2/26/83	2	24
	Even Now	3/19/83	4/30/83	18	15
	Roll Me Away	6/4/83	7/2/83	28	10
	Old Time Rock & Roll	10/8/83	11/12/83	5	17
	Understanding	11/3/84	12/8/84	20	14
	American Storm	3/15/86	4/19/86	11	12
	Like A Rock	5/24/86	6/28/86	21	10

Artist	Title	Debut	Peak	Pos	Wks
	It's You	8/16/86	9/13/86	39	7
	Shakedown	5/23/87	8/8/87	2	17
Sembello, Michael					
	Maniac	7/23/83	8/27/83	4	18
Sevelle, Taja					
	Love Is Contagious	9/12/87	10/10/87	26	6
Sexton, Charlie					
	Beat's So Lonely	2/22/86	3/29/86	13	10
Shalamar					
	The Second Time Around	3/1/80	3/29/80	15	13
	Dead Giveaway	10/15/83	11/12/83	24	10
	Dancing In The Sheets	5/19/84	6/16/84	13	13
Shannon					
	Let The Music Play	11/26/83	2/4/84	6	24
Shaw, Tommy					
	Girls With Guns	10/6/84	11/3/84	30	9
	Lonely School	1/19/85	2/2/85	41	6
	No Such Thing	11/14/87	11/28/87	34	3
	Ever Since The World Began	2/13/88	3/5/88	22	4
also see Styx					
Sheila E.					
	The Glamorous Life	8/25/84	10/13/84	4	17
	A Love Bizarre	2/8/86	3/1/86	12	10
Sheriff					
	When I'm With You	12/3/88	2/18/89	1	17
Shooting Star					
	Hollywood	3/6/82	4/17/82	32	12
Simmons, Patrick					
	So Wrong	5/14/83	6/4/83	24	9
also see the Doobie Brothers					
Simon, Carly					
	Jesse	10/4/80	11/29/80	5	19
	Coming Around Again	12/13/86	1/17/87	20	7

Artist	Title	Debut	Peak	Pos	Wks
Simon, Paul					
	Late In The Evening	8/9/80	9/20/80	12	18
	You Can Call Me Al	8/9/86	10/4/86	28	15
	You Can Call Me Al	4/4/87	5/30/87	8	13
Simple Minds					
	Don't You (Forget About Me)	3/30/85	6/1/85	2	17
	Alive & Kicking	10/19/85	12/21/85	8	20
	Sanctify Yourself	1/25/86	3/8/86	19	12
	All The Things She Said	5/3/86	5/31/86	28	7
Simply Red					
	Holding Back The Years	5/24/86	7/19/86	1	15
	Money$ Too Tight (To Mention)	8/16/86	9/6/86	26	8
	If You Don't Know Me By Now	6/3/89	7/15/89	2	13
Sister Carol					
	Wild Thing	2/7/87	3/7/87	29	5
Skid Row					
	Youth Gone Wild	5/13/89	6/24/89	14	10
	18 And Life	7/22/89	9/9/89	3	14
	I Remember You	10/28/89	1/13/90	2	26
Sly Fox					
	Let's Go All The Way	3/15/86	5/3/86	9	14
Smith, Frankie					
	Double Dutch Bus	8/15/81	8/29/81	26	9
Soft Cell					
	Tainted Love	2/6/82	5/1/82	9	34
S.O.S. Band					
	Take Your Time (Do It Right) Part 1	7/12/80	8/30/80	8	17
Soul II Soul					
	Keep On Movin'	9/2/89	9/16/89	14	5
	Back To Life (However Do You Want Me)	11/25/89	12/30/89	5	10
Souther, J.D.					
	You're Only Lonely	12/1/79	12/29/79	12	14

also see Taylor, James & J.D. Souther

Artist Title	Debut	Peak	Pos	Wks
Spandau Ballet				
True	10/1/83	10/29/83	5	16
Spinners				
Working My Way Back To You/Forgive Me, Girl	3/8/80	4/19/80	3	19
Cupid/I've Loved You For A Long Time	6/28/80	8/9/80	12	16
Springfield, Rick				
Jessie's Girl	6/20/81	8/1/81	1	27
I've Done Everything For You	10/10/81	11/28/81	7	18
Don't Talk To Strangers	3/20/82	6/12/82	6	24
What Kind Of Fool Am I	6/19/82	7/31/82	21	16
Affair Of The Heart	4/23/83	6/4/83	10	18
Human Touch	9/24/83	10/22/83	27	8
Love Somebody	4/7/84	5/12/84	14	12
Bop 'Til You Drop	9/15/84	10/13/84	26	10
Bruce	12/22/84	1/19/85	22	8
Rock Of Life	2/13/88	3/12/88	18	6
Springsteen, Bruce				
Hungry Heart	11/1/80	12/20/80	5	21
Dancing In The Dark	6/2/84	7/7/84	3	22
Cover Me	9/1/84	9/22/84	18	16
Born In The U.S.A.	11/24/84	1/12/85	10	17
I'm On Fire	3/2/85	4/6/85	8	18
Trapped	4/20/85	4/20/85	49	1
Glory Days	6/1/85	7/20/85	8	17
I'm Goin' Down	9/7/85	10/5/85	9	11
My Hometown	12/14/85	1/18/86	6	14
War	11/22/86	12/27/86	8	8
Squeeze				
Hourglass	9/19/87	10/31/87	20	8
also see Carrack, Paul				
Squier, Billy				
The Stroke	5/23/81	7/25/81	1	29
In The Dark	9/5/81	10/31/81	10	17
My Kinda Lover	11/21/81	12/19/81	19	13
Everybody Wants You	10/2/82	12/11/82	11	20

Artist Title	Debut	Peak	Pos	Wks
Stacey Q				
Two Of Hearts	8/23/86	10/18/86	1	18
We Connect	2/28/87	3/28/87	19	6
Stallone, Frank				
Far From Over	9/3/83	10/1/83	12	12
Stanley, Michael, Band				
He Can't Love You	1/17/81	2/28/81	9	16
Stansfield, Lisa				
All Around The World	3/31/90	5/5/90	2	6
also see Blue Zone U.K.				
Starr, Brenda K.				
I Still Believe	6/25/88	7/23/88	10	8
What You See Is What You Get	9/17/88	10/1/88	22	4
Stars On 45				
Stars On 45	5/16/81	6/13/81	2	18
Steely Dan				
Hey Nineteen	12/27/80	2/14/81	11	18
Time Out Of Mind	4/25/81	5/16/81	29	7
also see Fagen, Donald				
Steinman, Jim				
Rock And Roll Dreams Come Through	6/27/81	8/1/81	17	17
Stephenson, Van				
Modern Day Delilah	6/23/84	7/7/84	27	9
Stevie B				
Love Me For Life	2/17/90	3/10/90	11	9
Stewart, Jermaine				
We Don't Have To Take Our Clothes Off	6/21/86	8/9/86	4	15
Stewart, Rod				
Passion	12/20/80	1/24/81	15	15
Young Turks	11/21/81	1/16/82	3	19
Infatuation	6/30/84	7/21/84	14	12
Some Guys Have All The Luck	11/3/84	11/24/84	31	8
Love Touch	5/31/86	8/9/86	10	16
Forever Young	8/27/88	10/1/88	16	7

Artist	Title	Debut	Peak	Pos	Wks
	My Heart Can't Tell You No	3/4/89	4/1/89	12	6
	Crazy About Her	6/3/89	6/17/89	23	5

Sting
	If You Love Somebody Set Them Free	6/22/85	8/3/85	5	16
	Fortress Around Your Heart	8/24/85	10/12/85	12	14
	Love Is The Seventh Wave	11/9/85	12/14/85	20	12
	Russians	1/25/86	3/8/86	16	12
	We'll Be Together	10/10/87	11/28/87	10	11

also see the Police

Stray Cats
	Rock This Town	11/6/82	12/25/82	4	20
	Stray Cat Strut	1/15/83	2/19/83	4	18
	(She's) Sexy + 17	9/17/83	10/1/83	13	12

Streisand, Barbra & Donna Summer
	No More Tears (Enough Is Enough)	11/3/79	12/1/79	2	18

Streisand, Barbra
	Woman In Love	9/13/80	10/18/80	2	23
	Comin' In And Out Of Your Life	12/12/81	1/9/82	16	12

Streisand, Barbra & Barry Gibb
	Guilty	12/6/80	1/10/81	13	22

Streisand, Barbra & Don Johnson
	Till I Loved You	11/5/88	11/26/88	15	5

also see Gibb, Barry; Johnson, Don and Summer, Donna

Stryper
	Honestly	11/21/87	1/30/88	4	16

Styx
	Babe	10/6/79	11/24/79	1	26
	Why Me	12/15/79	2/2/80	21	16
	The Best Of Times	1/24/81	3/28/81	4	22
	Too Much Time On My Hands	3/21/81	5/9/81	4	18
	Mr. Roboto	2/5/83	3/12/83	1	26
	Don't Let It End	4/30/83	6/4/83	12	15

also see DeYoung, Dennis and Shaw, Tommy

Sugarhill Gang
	Rapper's Delight	11/10/79	12/22/79	17	18

Artist Title	Debut	Peak	Pos	Wks
Summer, Donna				
Dim All The Lights	9/29/79	11/24/79	12	18
On The Radio	2/2/80	3/15/80	5	18
The Wanderer	10/11/80	11/29/80	10	17
Love Is In Control (Finger On The Trigger)	8/14/82	9/11/82	11	13
She Works Hard For The Money	8/6/83	9/10/83	2	17
also see Streisand, Barbra & Donna Summer				
Supertramp				
Take The Long Way Home	11/17/79	12/29/79	10	14
. Dreamer	11/29/80	12/6/80	35	8
It's Raining Again	10/30/82	12/4/82	10	17
My Kind Of Lady	2/26/83	3/19/83	34	9
also see Hodgson, Roger				
Surface				
Happy	7/25/87	8/8/87	28	4
Shower Me With Your Love	8/12/89	9/16/89	6	10
Survivor				
Poor Man's Son	10/31/81	12/19/81	16	17
Summer Nights	2/6/82	3/20/82	30	12
Eye Of The Tiger	6/12/82	7/3/82	1	23
Caught In The Game	10/29/83	11/12/83	23	9
I Can't Hold Back	10/6/84	12/15/84	22	22
High On You	1/26/85	3/16/85	24	15
The Search Is Over	5/18/85	6/29/85	22	14
First Night	8/17/85	9/21/85	44	7
Burning Heart	11/2/85	2/1/86	14	20
Is This Love	11/1/86	12/27/86	36	11
Didn't Know It Was Love	10/1/88	10/22/88	24	5
Swayze, Patrick (featuring Wendy Fraser)				
She's Like The Wind	2/20/88	3/26/88	4	11
Sweat, Keith				
I Want Her	2/27/88	4/9/88	6	8
Sweet Sensation				
Sincerely Yours	4/1/89	4/29/89	10	6
Love Child	4/28/90	5/5/90	24	2

Artist Title	Debut	Peak	Pos	Wks
Swing Out Sister				
Breakout	10/10/87	11/21/87	6	9
Sylvia				
Nobody	11/13/82	11/27/82	19	14
System				
Don't Disturb This Groove	5/9/87	7/4/87	6	17
Ta Mara & the Seen				
Everybody Dance	1/11/86	2/8/86	26	9
Taco				
Puttin' On The Ritz	8/13/83	9/17/83	2	18
Talking Heads				
Burning Down The House	9/24/83	10/15/83	8	17
And She Was	10/19/85	11/23/85	14	11
Wild Wild Life	8/23/86	10/11/86	20	16
Love For Sale	1/24/87	2/14/87	27	4
also see Tom Tom Club				
Tami Show				
She's Only 20	2/27/88	4/2/88	22	6
Tarney/Spencer Band				
No Time To Lose	9/5/81	10/24/81	24	16
Taste Of Honey				
Sukiyaki	5/16/81	6/20/81	7	14
Taylor, James & J.D. Souther				
Her Town Too	3/21/81	5/2/81	20	15
Taylor, James				
Everyday	10/26/85	1/18/86	46	13
also see Souther, J.D.				
Tears For Fears				
Everybody Wants To Rule The World	4/13/85	6/29/85	1	20
Shout	6/29/85	7/27/85	1	16
Head Over Heels	9/14/85	10/19/85	11	14
Mothers Talk	5/10/86	5/31/86	24	6
Technotronic featuring Felly				
Pump Up The Jam	11/4/89	12/9/89	1	27

Artist	Title	Debut	Peak	Pos	Wks
Technotronic					
	Get Up (Before The Night Is Over)	2/24/90	4/21/90	1	11
.38 Special					
	Hold On Loosely	4/4/81	6/13/81	5	22
	Caught Up In You	5/15/82	7/17/82	11	23
	You Keep Runnin' Away	9/25/82	10/16/82	27	8
	If I'd Been The One	1/7/84	2/4/84	27	11
	Back Where You Belong	3/10/84	3/31/84	26	8
	Teacher Teacher	10/20/84	11/24/84	23	10
	Like No Other Night	5/10/86	6/28/86	32	11
	Second Chance	5/13/89	5/20/89	20	3
Thompson Twins					
	Hold Me Now	3/24/84	5/5/84	5	17
	Doctor! Doctor!	6/16/84	7/21/84	16	11
	Lay Your Hands On Me	9/28/85	11/16/85	11	17
	King For A Day	1/18/86	2/15/86	15	13
	Nothing In Common	7/26/86	9/13/86	29	9
	Get That Love	3/28/87	4/18/87	28	5
Thomson, Ali					
	Take A Little Rhythm	8/23/80	9/6/80	36	7
Tierra					
	Together	2/28/81	3/14/81	28	8
Tiffany					
	I Think We're Alone Now	8/15/87	10/31/87	1	21
	Could've Been	11/21/87	1/23/88	1	19
	I Saw Him Standing There	3/19/88	4/23/88	3	9
	All This Time	1/7/89	1/28/89	22	5
'Til Tuesday					
	Voices Carry	6/22/85	7/20/85	15	11
	What About Love	11/15/86	12/13/86	36	5
Timbuk 3					
	The Future's So Bright, I Gotta Wear Shades	11/29/86	1/10/87	15	7
Time					
	Jungle Love	2/9/85	3/16/85	6	14

Artist Title	Debut	Peak	Pos	Wks
Timex Social Club				
Rumors	8/2/86	8/30/86	4	13
Tom Tom Club				
Genius Of Love	3/13/82	4/17/82	18	14
also see Talking Heads				
Tommy Tutone				
867-5309/Jenny	3/6/82	4/17/82	5	23
Tone Loc				
Wild Thing	12/17/88	1/28/89	1	16
Funky Cold Medina	2/25/89	4/29/89	2	16
Tony! Toni! Tone!				
Little Walter	6/18/88	6/25/88	29	2
Toto				
Rosanna	5/8/82	7/3/82	3	22
Make Believe	8/14/82	10/16/82	25	12
Africa	11/13/82	1/15/83	3	24
I Won't Hold You Back	4/2/83	5/14/83	15	16
Stranger In Town	12/8/84	1/12/85	37	7
I'll Be Over You	8/30/86	11/29/86	25	18
Townshend, Pete				
Let My Love Open The Door	7/19/80	9/13/80	9	17
Face The Face	11/9/85	1/18/86	14	17
also see the Who				
T'Pau				
Heart And Soul	6/6/87	8/8/87	6	19
Trance Dance				
River Of Love	7/18/87	8/8/87	31	4
Traveling Wilburys				
Last Night	4/15/89	4/15/89	29	2
also see Electric Light Orchestra; Harrison, George and Petty, Tom				
Triumph				
Magic Power	10/24/81	12/12/81	14	15
Say Goodbye	2/20/82	4/24/82	43	13
Somebody's Out There	10/18/86	11/22/86	36	9

Artist	Title	Debut	Peak	Pos	Wks
Tubes					
	She's A Beauty	4/30/83	6/11/83	9	17
Turner, Tina					
	What's Love Got To Do With It	7/14/84	9/8/84	1	22
	Better Be Good To Me	9/22/84	11/10/84	11	20
	Private Dancer	3/23/85	4/20/85	23	8
	Show Some Respect	5/25/85	6/8/85	35	6
	We Don't Need Another Hero (Thunderdome)	7/6/85	8/31/85	3	17
	One Of The Living	10/12/85	11/23/85	22	11
	Typical Male	8/30/86	10/4/86	11	14
	Two People	12/27/86	1/10/87	55	3
	What You Get Is What You See	2/7/87	3/28/87	15	9
	also see Adams, Bryan & Tina Turner				
Twilley, Dwight					
	Girls	4/28/84	5/12/84	30	7
Twisted Sister					
	We're Not Gonna Take It	8/25/84	9/22/84	6	13
Tyler, Bonnie					
	Total Eclipse Of The Heart	9/10/83	10/8/83	1	21
UB40 with Chrissie Hynde					
	I Got You Babe	8/31/85	10/12/85	14	11
UB40					
	Red Red Wine	9/3/88	10/15/88	1	14
	also see the Pretenders				
Ullman, Tracy					
	They Don't Know	4/7/84	5/19/84	10	12
USA For Africa					
	We Are The World	3/23/85	3/30/85	1	18
U2					
	Pride (In The Name Of Love)	12/15/84	1/12/85	21	9
	With Or Without You	3/28/87	5/23/87	1	16
	I Still Haven't Found What I'm Looking For	6/13/87	8/15/87	3	17
	Where The Streets Have No Name	10/10/87	11/14/87	10	8
	Desire	10/15/88	11/26/88	2	13
	Angel Of Harlem	1/21/89	2/18/89	7	6

Artist Title	Debut	Peak	Pos	Wks
Van Halen				
(Oh) Pretty Woman	2/13/82	3/20/82	8	21
Jump	1/21/84	3/3/84	2	25
I'll Wait	4/21/84	6/2/84	24	14
Panama	7/28/84	8/18/84	23	9
Hot For Teacher	12/15/84	1/5/85	33	6
Why Can't This Be Love	3/22/86	4/19/86	4	14
Dreams	6/14/86	7/5/86	28	7
Black And Blue	5/21/88	6/11/88	18	5
When It's Love	7/30/68	9/10/88	7	10
also see Hagar, Sammy and Roth, David Lee				
Vandenberg				
Burning Heart	4/30/83	5/14/83	47	3
Vandross, Luther with Gregory Hines				
There's Nothing Better Than Love	4/18/87	5/9/87	30	5
Vandross, Luther				
Here And Now	3/3/90	4/14/90	4	10
Vangelis				
Chariots Of Fire - Titles	3/27/82	5/8/82	1	19
Vannelli, Gino				
Living Inside Myself	5/2/81	5/30/81	13	15
Vapors				
Turning Japanese	9/27/80	11/22/80	4	21
Vega, Suzanne				
Luka	6/20/87	8/15/87	2	18
Vera, Billy & the Beaters				
At This Moment	11/29/86	1/24/87	1	14
I Can Take Care Of Myself	2/7/87	3/7/87	28	5
Wagner, Jack				
All I Need	12/8/84	1/19/85	3	15
Weatherman Says	4/11/87	6/6/87	17	12
Waite, John				
Missing You	7/21/84	9/15/84	3	20
Every Step Of The Way	8/10/85	9/28/85	25	12

Artist	Title	Debut	Peak	Pos	Wks
	If Anybody Had A Heart	7/5/86	8/9/86	39	6
also see Bad English					

Walsh, Joe

	All Night Long	7/12/80	8/9/80	22	13
	A Life Of Illusion	5/30/81	7/11/81	17	15
also see the Eagles					

Wang Chung

	Dance Hall Days	7/21/84	8/11/84	11	9
	To Live And Die In L.A.	11/23/85	1/11/86	25	12
	Everybody Have Fun Tonight	10/25/86	12/27/86	4	16
	Let's Go	2/14/87	4/25/87	4	12

Warrant

	Down Boys	5/20/89	7/1/89	10	13
	Heaven	7/15/89	9/23/89	2	17
	Big Talk	11/18/89	11/18/89	25	1
	Sometimes She Cries	11/25/89	3/10/90	7	16

Warwick, Dionne

	Deja Vu	12/29/79	2/2/80	15	13
	No Night So Long	10/4/80	10/25/80	27	9
	Heartbreaker	11/27/82	1/8/83	14	14
	Take The Short Way Home	4/9/83	4/30/83	31	6

Dionne & Friends

	That's What Friends Are For	12/14/85	2/22/86	1	19

Warwick, Dionne & Jeffrey Osborne

	Love Power	7/25/87	9/5/87	13	9
also see John, Elton; Knight, Gladys; Osborne, Jeffrey and Wonder, Stevie					

Was (Not Was)

	Walk The Dinosaur	1/21/89	3/18/89	8	12

Washington, Jr., Grover & Bill Withers

	Just The Two Of Us	3/28/81	5/16/81	8	17

Waterfront

	Cry	4/15/89	4/29/89	26	4

Watley, Jody

	Looking For A New Love	3/7/87	5/9/87	1	19
	Don't You Want Me	11/14/87	12/19/87	14	7

Artist	Title	Debut	Peak	Pos	Wks
	Real Love	4/1/89	5/20/89	8	10
	Everything	12/9/89	1/13/90	11	12

Watley, Jody with Eric B. & Rakim

	Friends	8/26/89	9/2/89	16	3

Wax

	Right Between The Eyes	5/10/86	5/31/86	27	6
	Bridge To Your Heart	3/12/88	4/16/88	22	6

Wham!

	Wake Me Up Before You Go-Go	10/13/84	11/10/84	1	18
	Careless Whisper	1/19/85	2/16/85	1	20
	Everything She Wants	3/23/85	5/11/85	11	19
	Freedom	7/20/85	8/24/85	23	15
	I'm Your Man	11/30/85	2/1/86	9	17
	The Edge Of Heaven	7/5/86	8/2/86	14	11

also see Estus, Deon with George Michael and Michael, George

When In Rome

	The Promise	10/22/88	11/12/88	25	6

Whispers

	And The Beat Goes On	3/22/80	4/12/80	23	11
	Rock Steady	6/27/87	8/15/87	7	16

White, Karyn

	The Way You Love Me	12/10/88	12/31/88	13	5
	Superwoman	2/25/89	4/1/89	8	7
	Secret Rendezvous	8/5/89	8/26/89	15	6

also see Lorber, Jeff featuring Karyn White

White Lion

	Wait	3/5/88	5/14/88	1	18
	When The Children Cry	12/10/88	2/4/89	5	11

Whitesnake

	Here I Go Again	7/25/87	9/19/87	1	19
	Is This Love	11/21/87	1/9/88	4	12

Who

	You Better You Bet	3/21/81	5/2/81	2	18
	Athena	9/4/82	10/9/82	11	15

also see Daltrey, Roger and Townshend, Pete

Artist Title	Debut	Peak	Pos	Wks
Wiedlin, Jane				
Blue Kiss	10/12/85	11/16/85	34	8
Rush Hour	5/14/88	6/25/88	15	7
also see the Go-Go's				
Wilde, Kim				
You Keep Me Hangin' On	4/11/87	6/13/87	2	16
Say You Really Want Me	7/18/87	8/15/87	30	6
Wilder, Matthew				
Break My Stride	12/10/83	1/28/84	1	18
Will To Power				
Baby, I Love Your Way/Freebird Medley (Free Baby)	10/22/88	12/17/88	4	14
Williams, Deniece				
Let's Hear It For The Boy	4/21/84	6/2/84	1	17
Willis, Bruce				
Respect Yourself	12/27/86	3/14/87	8	13
Young Blood	4/4/87	4/25/87	31	5
Wilson, Ann & Robin Zander				
Surrender To Me	3/4/89	3/18/89	22	3
also see Cheap Trick; Heart and Reno, Mike & Ann Wilson				
Winger				
Headed For A Heartbreak	6/24/89	7/29/89	8	8
Winwood, Steve				
While You See A Chance	3/7/81	4/18/81	6	18
Arc Of A Diver	7/11/81	8/8/81	33	9
Higher Love	6/14/86	8/16/86	7	21
Freedom Overspill	9/27/86	10/18/86	41	7
The Finer Things	4/11/87	5/2/87	18	5
Back In The High Life Again	7/25/87	8/15/87	23	5
Roll With It	6/11/88	8/6/88	1	14
Holding On	12/24/88	1/14/89	18	5
Wolf, Peter				
Lights Out	8/11/84	9/1/84	20	11
Come As You Are	2/28/87	4/18/87	11	8
also see Geils, J., Band				

Artist	Title	Debut	Peak	Pos	Wks
Wonder, Stevie					
	Send One Your Love	12/1/79	1/19/80	20	13
	Master Blaster (Jammin')	10/11/80	11/29/80	9	18
	That Girl	3/13/82	4/10/82	9	15
	Do I Do	8/14/82	9/4/82	31	6
	I Just Called To Say I Love You	9/15/84	10/6/84	1	20
	Love Light In Flight	1/5/85	1/26/85	34	7
	Part-Time Lover	9/7/85	11/2/85	4	19
	Go Home	11/23/85	1/18/86	25	14
	Overjoyed	3/1/86	4/19/86	20	11

also see McCartney, Paul with Stevie Wonder and (Warwick), Dionne & Friends

Artist	Title	Debut	Peak	Pos	Wks
World Party					
	Ship Of Fools (Save Me From Tomorrow)	3/14/87	4/4/87	24	5
Wright, Gary					
	Really Wanna Know You	8/29/81	9/26/81	20	9
XTC					
	Generals And Majors	3/28/81	4/11/81	29	9
X2					
	Strange But True	3/19/88	4/30/88	22	8
Yankovic, "Weird Al"					
	Eat It	3/17/84	4/14/84	3	14
Yarbrough & Peoples					
	Don't Stop The Music	3/14/81	4/11/81	19	13
Yello					
	Oh Yeah	7/4/87	9/26/87	4	19
Yes					
	Owner Of A Lonely Heart	11/26/83	1/7/84	4	21

also see Asia and GTR

Artist	Title	Debut	Peak	Pos	Wks
Young, Paul					
	Come Back And Stay	4/21/84	5/26/84	22	12
	Everytime You Go Away	5/25/85	7/20/85	14	19
	I'm Gonna Tear Your Playhouse Down	9/14/85	10/26/85	19	11

also see Mike + the Mechanics

Artist	Title	Debut	Peak	Pos	Wks
Young MC					
	Bust A Move	10/14/89	11/11/89	1	14
Zappa, Frank					
	Valley Girl	6/26/82	7/10/82	42	3
ZZ Top					
	Gimme All Your Lovin	4/23/83	5/21/83	20	18
	Legs	6/16/84	7/14/84	8	15
	Sleeping Bag	10/19/85	11/23/85	12	16
	Stages	1/18/86	2/15/86	25	12
	Rough Boy	3/29/86	5/3/86	33	8
	Velcro Fly	8/2/86	9/6/86	46	7

ALPHABETICAL LISTING BY TITLE

Debut	Peak	Title	Artist	Pos	Wks
9/12/81	9/12/81	Abacab	Genesis	49	1
12/19/81	1/30/82	Abacab	Genesis	14	14
6/19/82	8/28/82	Abracadabra	Steve Miller Band	2	25
4/12/86	5/10/86	Absolute Beginners	David Bowie	29	8
3/1/86	5/10/86	Addicted To Love	Robert Palmer	1	18
2/18/84	3/24/84	Adult Education	Daryl Hall & John Oates	19	15
4/23/83	6/4/83	Affair Of The Heart	Rick Springfield	10	18
11/13/82	1/15/83	Africa	Toto	3	24
7/23/83	8/13/83	After The Fall	Journey	35	14
11/9/85	11/23/85	After The Fire	Roger Daltrey	30	5
3/10/84	4/7/84	Against All Odds (Take A Look At Me Now)	Phil Collins	2	21
5/31/80	7/12/80	Against The Wind	Bob Seger	4	17
2/7/81	4/4/81	Ah! Leah!	Donnie Iris	7	17
12/24/83	1/28/84	Ain't Nobody	Rufus & Chaka Khan	18	15
7/2/88	7/16/88	Airhead	Thomas Dolby	25	4
7/28/84	8/25/84	Alibis	Sergio Mendes	13	10
10/19/85	12/21/85	Alive & Kicking	Simple Minds	8	20
3/31/90	5/5/90	All Around The World	Lisa Stansfield	2	6
10/11/86	11/15/86	All Cried Out	Lisa Lisa & Cult Jam with Full Force	4	14
7/16/88	8/13/88	All Fired Up	Pat Benatar	20	5
12/8/84	1/19/85	All I Need	Jack Wagner	3	15
3/22/86	5/24/86	All I Need Is A Miracle	Mike + the Mechanics	13	16
4/21/90	5/5/90	All I Wanna Do Is Make Love To You	Heart	13	3
12/20/86	1/10/87	All I Wanted	Kansas	45	4
7/12/80	8/9/80	All Night Long	Joe Walsh	22	13
10/15/83	11/26/83	All Night Long (All Night)	Lionel Richie	1	24
7/28/84	8/18/84	All Of You	Julio Iglesias & Diana Ross	11	14
1/13/90	2/24/90	All Or Nothing	Milli Vanilli	5	13
8/16/80	10/4/80	All Out Of Love	Air Supply	3	27
8/9/80	10/11/80	All Over The World	Electric Light Orchestra	6	17
2/12/83	3/5/83	All Right	Christopher Cross	16	13

Debug	Peak	Title	Artist	Pos	Wks
12/31/88	2/4/89	All She Wants Is	Duran Duran	9	8
3/2/85	4/20/85	All She Wants To Do Is Dance	Don Henley	13	16
3/8/86	3/29/86	All The Kings Horses	Firm	38	5
6/28/86	8/23/86	All The Love In The World	Outfield	33	11
5/3/86	5/31/86	All The Things She Said	Simple Minds	28	7
1/7/89	1/28/89	All This Time	Tiffany	22	5
5/23/81	6/20/81	All Those Years Ago	George Harrison	3	14
10/27/84	12/15/84	All Through The Night	Cyndi Lauper	11	15
1/22/83	2/19/83	Allentown	Billy Joel	17	14
3/17/90	3/31/90	Almost Hear You Sigh	Rolling Stones	21	4
6/9/84	7/7/84	Almost Paradise... Love Theme From Footloose	Mike Reno & Ann Wilson	12	12
5/30/87	7/18/87	Alone	Heart	1	20
2/23/85	4/13/85	Along Comes A Woman	Chicago	26	12
6/11/88	7/2/88	Alphabet St.	Prince	11	5
4/14/90	5/5/90	Alright	Janet Jackson	9	4
4/18/87	6/6/87	Always	Atlantic Starr	1	15
6/5/82	7/3/82	Always On My Mind	Willie Nelson	6	22
4/9/88	5/14/88	Always On My Mind	Pet Shop Boys	4	9
5/28/83	7/9/83	Always Something There To Remind Me	Naked Eyes	5	15
10/4/86	11/8/86	Amanda	Boston	1	16
5/23/81	6/20/81	America	Neil Diamond	24	10
3/15/80	4/5/80	American Dream, An	Dirt Band	25	9
8/14/82	9/11/82	American Music	Pointer Sisters	24	9
3/15/86	4/19/86	American Storm	Bob Seger & the Silver Bullet Band	11	12
10/19/85	11/23/85	And She Was	Talking Heads	14	11
3/22/80	4/12/80	And The Beat Goes On	Whispers	23	11
9/28/85	11/2/85	And We Danced	Hooters	14	11
3/26/88	4/23/88	Angel	Aerosmith	7	12
4/27/85	6/15/85	Angel	Madonna	7	15
8/19/89	9/30/89	Angel Eyes	Jeff Healey Band	3	12
1/21/89	2/18/89	Angel Of Harlem	U2	7	6
4/4/81	5/30/81	Angel Of The Morning	Juice Newton	5	21
10/7/89	12/2/89	Angelia	Richard Marx	3	15
10/17/87	12/12/87	Animal	Def Leppard	12	11
6/29/85	7/27/85	Animal Instinct	Commodores	45	5
2/9/80	3/22/80	Another Brick In The Wall (Part II)	Pink Floyd	1	27

Debut	Peak	Title	Artist	Pos	Wks
11/11/89	12/16/89	Another Day In Paradise	Phil Collins	2	16
1/18/86	3/29/86	Another Night	Aretha Franklin	23	14
9/6/80	9/27/80	Another One Bites The Dust	Queen	1	30
9/17/88	10/1/88	Another Part Of Me	Michael Jackson	25	4
4/5/80	5/10/80	Any Way You Want It	Journey	17	18
4/16/88	5/21/88	Anything For You	Gloria Estefan & Miami Sound Machine	5	10
7/11/81	8/8/81	Arc Of A Diver	Steve Winwood	33	9
8/25/84	10/20/84	Are We Ourselves	Fixx	8	14
11/19/88	12/31/88	Armageddon It	Def Leppard	5	13
9/5/81	10/17/81	Arthur's Theme (Best That You Can Do)	Christopher Cross	3	21
11/29/86	1/24/87	At This Moment	Billy Vera & the Beaters	1	14
9/4/82	10/9/82	Athena	Who	11	15
4/14/84	5/12/84	Authority Song	John Cougar Mellencamp	17	12
2/25/84	5/5/84	Automatic	Pointer Sisters	7	18
4/6/85	6/1/85	Axel F	Harold Faltermeyer	1	20
1/26/80	2/9/80	Ayatollah	Steve Dahl & Teenage Radiation	12	16
10/6/79	11/24/79	Babe	Styx	1	26
12/25/82	1/29/83	Baby, Come To Me	Patti Austin with James Ingram	1	20
5/13/89	7/1/89	Baby Don't Forget My Number	Milli Vanilli	1	16
10/22/88	12/17/88	Baby, I Love Your Way/Freebird Medley (Free Baby)	Will To Power	4	14
8/9/86	9/27/86	Baby Love	Regina	9	13
2/9/80	3/15/80	Baby Talks Dirty	Knack	11	13
5/9/87	5/23/87	Back And Forth	Cameo	32	4
2/14/81	3/21/81	Back In Black	AC/DC	11	17
7/25/87	8/15/87	Back In The High Life Again	Steve Winwood	23	5
11/9/85	11/9/85	Back In Time	Huey Lewis & the News	46	1
1/22/83	2/26/83	Back On The Chain Gang	Pretenders	7	19
11/25/89	12/30/89	Back To Life (However Do You Want Me)	Soul II Soul	5	10
3/10/84	3/31/84	Back Where You Belong	.38 Special	26	8
9/12/87	11/7/87	Bad	Michael Jackson	8	13
3/15/86	4/26/86	Bad Boy	Miami Sound Machine	16	15
2/5/83	2/26/83	Bad Boy	Ray Parker, Jr.	23	8

Debut	Peak	Title	Artist	Pos	Wks
9/24/88	10/29/88	Bad Medicine	Bon Jovi	3	10
1/17/87	2/21/87	Ballerina Girl	Lionel Richie	3	9
1/24/87	3/28/87	Battleship Chains	Georgia Satellites	20	10
4/12/86	5/17/86	Be Good To Yourself	Journey	21	11
11/6/82	11/27/82	Be My Lady	Jefferson Starship	30	10
9/28/85	11/16/85	Be Near Me	ABC	17	12
8/29/81	9/26/81	Beach Boys Medley, The	Beach Boys	16	12
4/2/83	5/7/83	Beat It	Michael Jackson	1	25
4/17/82	5/15/82	Beatles' Movie Medley, The	Beatles	13	11
2/22/86	3/29/86	Beat's So Lonely	Charlie Sexton	13	10
2/6/88	3/12/88	Because Of You	Cover Girls	15	8
4/25/81	6/6/81	Being With You	Smokey Robinson	7	15
1/24/81	3/28/81	Best Of Times, The	Styx	4	22
5/2/81	5/30/81	Bette Davis Eyes	Kim Carnes	1	22
9/22/84	11/10/84	Better Be Good To Me	Tina Turner	11	20
12/17/88	1/21/89	Big Fun	Inner City	8	9
8/20/83	10/1/83	Big Log	Robert Plant	20	18
3/28/87	5/16/87	Big Love	Fleetwood Mac	9	11
11/16/85	12/21/85	Big Money, The	Rush	39	6
11/18/89	11/18/89	Big Talk	Warrant	25	1
11/22/86	3/14/87	Big Time	Peter Gabriel	6	19
5/3/80	6/21/80	Biggest Part Of Me	Ambrosia	9	20
2/12/83	3/26/83	Billie Jean	Michael Jackson	1	29
2/28/87	4/4/87	Bizarre Love Triangle	New Order	13	7
5/21/88	6/11/88	Black And Blue	Van Halen	18	5
2/24/90	3/31/90	Black Velvet	Alannah Myles	1	11
10/28/89	11/25/89	Blame It On The Rain	Milli Vanilli	2	17
9/22/84	11/3/84	Blue Jean	David Bowie	7	14
10/12/85	11/16/85	Blue Kiss	Jane Wiedlin	34	8
4/3/82	4/24/82	Bobbie Sue	Oak Ridge Boys	21	11
5/15/82	6/19/82	Body Language	Queen	9	16
3/7/87	4/11/87	Boom Boom (Let's Go Back To My Room)	Paul Lekakis	8	12
9/15/84	10/13/84	Bop 'Til You Drop	Rick Springfield	26	10
6/30/84	7/28/84	Borderline	Madonna	4	15
11/24/84	1/12/85	Born In The U.S.A.	Bruce Springsteen	10	17
12/3/88	1/21/89	Born To Be My Baby	Bon Jovi	4	14
8/9/80	9/6/80	Boulevard	Jackson Browne	10	15

Debut	Peak	Title	Artist	Pos	Wks
7/4/81	8/8/81	Boy From New York City	Manhattan Transfer	10	18
9/14/85	11/2/85	Boy In The Box	Corey Hart	21	12
10/29/88	11/26/88	Boy, I've Been Told	Sa-Fire	10	8
9/26/87	11/7/87	Boys Night Out	Timothy B. Schmit	27	8
1/12/85	2/2/85	Boys Of Summer, The	Don Henley	9	12
1/17/87	3/14/87	Brand New Lover	Dead Or Alive	3	12
4/12/80	5/24/80	Brass In Pocket (I'm Special)	Pretenders	4	22
3/21/87	5/2/87	Brass Monkey	Beastie Boys	21	8
12/10/83	1/28/84	Break My Stride	Matthew Wilder	1	18
3/12/88	4/30/88	Breakaway	Big Pig	15	9
5/19/84	6/16/84	Breakdance	Irene Cara	10	13
5/17/80	6/7/80	Breakdown Dead Ahead	Boz Scaggs	25	10
7/21/84	8/11/84	Breakin'...There's No Stopping Us	Ollie & Jerry	10	10
2/19/83	3/19/83	Breaking Us In Two	Joe Jackson	22	11
10/10/87	11/21/87	Breakout	Swing Out Sister	6	9
7/25/81	9/26/81	Breakup Song (They Don't Write 'Em), The	Greg Kihn Band	10	19
3/12/88	4/16/88	Bridge To Your Heart	Wax UK	22	6
5/27/89	7/8/89	Bring Me Edelweiss	Edelweiss	5	10
11/17/79	12/15/79	Broken Hearted Me	Anne Murray	24	10
10/5/85	12/14/85	Broken Wings	Mr. Mister	3	20
12/22/84	1/19/85	Bruce	Rick Springfield	22	8
5/6/89	6/17/89	Buffalo Stance	Neneh Cherry	1	16
8/8/81	10/24/81	Burnin' For You	Blue Oyster Cult	15	19
9/18/82	10/16/82	Burning Down One Side	Robert Plant	23	10
9/24/83	10/15/83	Burning Down The House	Talking Heads	8	17
11/2/85	2/1/86	Burning Heart	Survivor	14	20
4/30/83	5/14/83	Burning Heart	Vandenberg	47	3
10/14/89	11/11/89	Bust A Move	Young MC	1	14
10/18/86	11/22/86	California Dreamin'	Beach Boys	44	8
1/19/85	2/23/85	California Girls	David Lee Roth	5	16
9/2/89	10/28/89	Call It Love	Poco	11	10
3/8/80	4/12/80	Call Me	Blondie	1	27
3/15/86	4/19/86	Call Me	Dennis DeYoung	44	7
1/5/85	2/9/85	Call To The Heart	Giuffria	11	11
2/15/86	3/29/86	Calling America	Electric Light Orchestra	22	12
11/28/87	1/16/88	Candle In The Wind	Elton John	9	9

Debut	Peak	Title	Artist	Pos	Wks
1/19/85	3/16/85	Can't Fight This Feeling	REO Speedwagon	3	19
5/14/83	6/11/83	Can't Find Love	Jefferson Starship	36	8
12/20/86	2/14/87	Can't Help Falling In Love	Corey Hart	20	11
8/15/87	9/19/87	Can't We Try	Dan Hill with Vonda Sheppard	12	12
2/21/87	4/18/87	Can'tcha Say (You Believe In Me)/Still In Love	Boston	14	11
8/16/86	9/27/86	Captain Of Her Heart, The	Double	14	12
1/19/85	2/16/85	Careless Whisper	Wham!	1	20
9/29/84	11/24/84	Caribbean Queen (No More Love On The Run)	Billy Ocean	3	19
8/22/87	10/3/87	Carrie	Europe	5	13
4/19/80	5/31/80	Cars	Gary Numan	5	20
9/19/87	10/24/87	Casanova	Levert	14	9
11/7/87	12/12/87	Catch Me (I'm Falling)	Pretty Poison	4	15
10/29/83	11/12/83	Caught In The Game	Survivor	23	9
5/15/82	7/17/82	Caught Up In You	.38 Special	11	23
9/12/87	11/7/87	Causing A Commotion	Madonna	4	13
12/20/80	3/7/81	Celebration	Kool & the Gang	2	41
5/25/85	6/22/85	Centerfield	John Fogerty	37	9
12/5/81	1/16/82	Centerfold	J. Geils Band	1	27
11/8/86	1/24/87	C'est La Vie	Robbie Nevil	3	17
8/6/88	9/3/88	Chains Of Love	Erasure	19	5
10/22/88	11/5/88	Chains Of Love	Erasure	16	3
11/15/86	11/22/86	Change In The Weather	John Fogerty	46	4
12/13/86	2/14/87	Change Of Heart	Cyndi Lauper	10	11
3/19/83	4/16/83	Change Of Heart	Tom Petty & the Heartbreakers	19	11
3/27/82	5/8/82	Chariots Of Fire - Titles	Vangelis	1	19
8/10/85	10/5/85	Cherish	Kool & the Gang	1	20
4/15/89	4/15/89	Cherish	Madonna	30	2
8/26/89	9/9/89	Cherish	Madonna	18	5
11/28/87	1/9/88	Cherry Bomb	John Cougar Mellencamp	7	10
5/5/90	5/5/90	Children Of The Night	Richard Marx	28	1
11/5/83	12/3/83	Church Of The Poison Mind	Culture Club	11	17
4/30/88	6/18/88	Circle In The Sand	Belinda Carlisle	6	10
8/31/85	9/21/85	C-I-T-Y	John Cafferty & the Beaver Brown Band	35	7
11/21/81	12/19/81	Closer To The Heart	Rush	20	12
3/3/90	3/31/90	C'mon And Get My Love	D-Mob	7	10

Debut	Peak	Title	Artist	Pos	Wks
7/15/89	8/26/89	Cold Hearted	Paula Abdul	3	16
2/28/87	4/18/87	Come As You Are	Peter Wolf	11	8
4/21/84	5/26/84	Come Back And Stay	Paul Young	22	12
5/28/83	7/30/83	Come Dancing	Kinks	5	18
1/23/82	2/13/82	Come Go With Me	Beach Boys	31	6
2/28/87	4/11/87	Come Go With Me	Expose	2	8
2/12/83	4/9/83	Come On Eileen	Dexys Midnight Runners	3	20
10/24/87	11/21/87	Come On, Let's Go	Los Lobos	16	6
11/10/79	12/1/79	Come To Me	France Joli	18	11
12/12/81	1/9/82	Comin' In And Out Of Your Life	Barbra Streisand	16	12
12/13/86	1/17/87	Coming Around Again	Carly Simon	20	7
4/26/80	6/28/80	Coming Up (Live At Glasgow)	Paul McCartney & Wings	1	24
1/18/86	3/1/86	Conga	Miami Sound Machine	3	14
11/22/86	1/24/87	Control	Janet Jackson	6	13
12/22/79	1/26/80	Cool Change	Little River Band	24	11
11/3/84	12/22/84	Cool It Now	New Edition	1	20
1/16/82	2/27/82	Cool Night	Paul Davis	17	14
11/21/87	1/23/88	Could've Been	Tiffany	1	19
9/16/89	11/11/89	Cover Girl	New Kids On The Block	2	14
9/1/84	9/22/84	Cover Me	Bruce Springsteen	18	16
12/15/79	1/26/80	Coward Of The County	Kenny Rogers	2	22
11/14/87	12/12/87	Crazy	Icehouse	21	5
1/30/82	3/6/82	Crazy (Keep On Falling)	John Hall Band	18	11
6/3/89	6/17/89	Crazy About Her	Rod Stewart	23	5
3/16/85	4/13/85	Crazy For You	Madonna	2	19
1/26/80	3/8/80	Crazy Little Thing Called Love	Queen	1	22
8/8/81	9/5/81	Crazy Train	Ozzy Osbourne	19	11
5/22/82	6/12/82	Crimson And Clover	Joan Jett & the Blackhearts	14	15
5/30/87	8/1/87	Cross My Broken Heart	Jets	19	12
9/8/84	10/6/84	Cruel Summer	Bananarama	7	12
1/26/80	3/1/80	Cruisin'	Smokey Robinson	14	14
11/12/83	12/10/83	Crumblin' Down	John Cougar Mellencamp	17	12
5/17/86	6/28/86	Crush On You	Jets	2	13
8/24/85	9/21/85	Cry	Godley & Creme	13	12
4/15/89	4/29/89	Cry	Waterfront	26	4
2/7/87	3/21/87	Cry Wolf	a-ha	22	7
3/7/81	4/4/81	Crying	Don McLean	15	12

Debut	Peak	Title	Artist	Pos	Wks
3/25/89	5/6/89	Cult Of Personality	Living Colour	2	13
9/17/83	10/29/83	Cum On Feel The Noize	Quiet Riot	3	22
6/28/80	8/9/80	Cupid/I've Loved You For A Long Time	Spinners	12	16
11/12/83	12/17/83	Curly Shuffle, The	Jump 'n the Saddle	1	19
6/25/83	7/23/83	Cuts Like A Knife	Bryan Adams	22	11
3/21/87	4/18/87	Dance	Ratt	23	5
7/21/84	8/11/84	Dance Hall Days	Wang Chung	11	9
9/24/88	10/22/88	Dance Little Sister (Part One)	Terence Trent D'Arby	15	6
6/24/89	7/22/89	Dancing In Heaven (Orbital Be-Bop)	Q-Feel	16	7
6/2/84	7/7/84	Dancing In The Dark	Bruce Springsteen	3	22
5/19/84	6/16/84	Dancing In The Sheets	Shalamar	13	13
8/31/85	9/28/85	Dancing In The Street	Mick Jagger & David Bowie	4	15
7/19/86	9/13/86	Dancing On The Ceiling	Lionel Richie	4	17
5/31/86	7/26/86	Danger Zone	Kenny Loggins	8	14
1/20/90	3/17/90	Dangerous	Roxette	2	16
7/27/85	9/21/85	Dare Me	Pointer Sisters	20	16
11/3/84	11/24/84	Darling Nikki	Prince	46	5
2/1/86	3/1/86	Day By Day	Hooters	34	7
5/2/87	5/23/87	Day-In Day-Out	David Bowie	24	5
12/6/80	1/24/81	De Do Do Do, De Da Da Da	Police	7	20
10/15/83	11/12/83	Dead Giveaway	Shalamar	24	10
4/15/89	5/27/89	Dear Jesse	Madonna	16	7
12/13/86	2/21/87	Deep River Woman	Lionel Richie with Alabama	3	14
12/29/79	2/2/80	Deja Vu	Dionne Warwick	15	13
10/15/83	11/12/83	Delirious	Prince	10	15
3/5/83	5/7/83	Der Kommissar	After The Fire	8	20
9/15/84	10/27/84	Desert Moon	Dennis DeYoung	15	15
2/23/80	3/22/80	Desire	Andy Gibb	24	10
10/15/88	11/26/88	Desire	U2	2	13
3/26/88	4/23/88	Devil Inside	INXS	6	10
8/11/79	9/22/79	Devil Went Down To Georgia, The	Charlie Daniels Band	2	23
1/21/89	2/11/89	Dial My Heart	Boys	13	6
5/2/87	6/20/87	Diamonds	Herb Alpert	6	13
9/23/89	11/11/89	Didn't I (Blow Your Mind)	New Kids On The Block	4	10
10/1/88	10/22/88	Didn't Know It Was Love	Survivor	24	5

Debut	Peak	Title	Artist	Pos	Wks
8/15/87	9/26/87	Didn't We Almost Have It All	Whitney Houston	2	16
3/21/87	5/2/87	(I Just) Died In Your Arms	Cutting Crew	1	17
6/7/86	7/5/86	Digging Your Scene	Blow Monkeys	26	10
9/29/79	11/24/79	Dim All The Lights	Donna Summer	12	18
5/7/88	6/25/88	Dirty Diana	Michael Jackson	1	15
10/30/82	12/4/82	Dirty Laundry	Don Henley	3	21
8/14/82	9/4/82	Do I Do	Stevie Wonder	31	6
10/26/85	12/7/85	Do It For Love	Sheena Easton	33	10
12/8/79	2/16/80	Do That To Me One More Time	Captain & Tennille	5	21
1/5/85	1/12/85	Do They Know It's Christmas	Band Aid	1	9
1/19/85	2/9/85	Do What You Do	Jermaine Jackson	20	9
3/6/82	5/8/82	Do You Believe In Love	Huey Lewis & the News	11	20
6/11/88	7/9/88	Do You Love Me	Contours	14	6
1/19/80	2/16/80	Do You Love What You Feel	Rufus & Chaka Khan	26	9
1/29/83	3/5/83	Do You Really Want To Hurt Me	Culture Club	3	20
9/8/79	10/6/79	Do You Think I'm Disco	Steve Dahl & Teenage Radiation	5	19
9/11/82	10/16/82	Do You Wanna Touch Me (Oh Yeah)	Joan Jett & the Blackhearts	11	13
3/12/88	3/12/88	(Sittin' On) Dock Of The Bay, The	Michael Bolton	25	2
6/16/84	7/21/84	Doctor! Doctor!	Thompson Twins	16	11
8/1/87	9/19/87	Doing It All For My Baby	Huey Lewis & the News	19	8
4/7/84	5/5/84	Don't Answer Me	Alan Parsons Project	21	11
8/2/80	9/13/80	Don't Ask Me Why	Billy Joel	21	14
9/10/88	10/29/88	Don't Be Cruel	Bobby Brown	13	8
9/10/88	10/22/88	Don't Be Cruel	Cheap Trick	5	8
8/4/79	10/13/79	Don't Bring Me Down	Electric Light Orchestra	5	24
10/21/89	11/11/89	Don't Close Your Eyes	Kix	19	4
4/6/85	5/11/85	Don't Come Around Here No More	Tom Petty & the Heartbreakers	12	12
7/30/83	9/17/83	Don't Cry	Asia	8	15
5/9/87	7/4/87	Don't Disturb This Groove	System	6	17
12/22/79	2/9/80	Don't Do Me Like That	Tom Petty & the Heartbreakers	6	21
1/17/87	4/25/87	Don't Dream It's Over	Crowded House	1	20
4/19/80	5/31/80	Don't Fall In Love With A Dreamer	Kenny Rogers with Kim Carnes	7	19
8/28/82	10/16/82	Don't Fight It	Kenny Loggins with Steve Perry	5	18

Debut	Peak	Title	Artist	Pos	Wks
8/2/86	10/25/86	Don't Forget Me (When I'm Gone)	Glass Tiger	5	18
10/11/86	11/22/86	Don't Get Me Wrong	Pretenders	21	14
4/18/87	4/25/87	Don't Give Up	Peter Gabriel & Kate Bush	36	3
11/11/89	12/16/89	Don't Know Much	Linda Ronstadt featuring Aaron Neville	4	16
10/8/88	11/19/88	Don't Know What You Got (Till It's Gone)	Cinderella	6	9
1/17/87	3/7/87	Don't Leave Me This Way	Communards	15	9
12/1/79	12/29/79	Don't Let Go	Isaac Hayes	18	15
6/13/81	7/25/81	Don't Let Him Go	REO Speedwagon	25	12
1/30/82	3/20/82	Don't Let Him Know	Prism	22	15
4/30/83	6/4/83	Don't Let It End	Styx	12	15
10/3/87	10/3/87	Don't Look Down - The Sequel	Go West	41	1
7/6/85	9/7/85	Don't Lose My Number	Phil Collins	9	18
5/30/87	8/29/87	Don't Mean Nothing	Richard Marx	6	19
1/17/87	2/14/87	Don't Need A Gun	Billy Idol	35	5
5/28/83	6/25/83	Don't Pay The Ferryman	Chris DeBurgh	23	10
12/10/88	1/28/89	Don't Rush Me	Taylor Dayne	3	11
1/23/88	2/20/88	Don't Shed A Tear	Paul Carrack	8	6
11/18/89	12/9/89	Don't Shut Me Out	Kevin Paige	23	5
2/21/81	4/4/81	Don't Stand So Close To Me	Police	8	19
10/25/86	12/6/86	Don't Stand So Close To Me '86	Police	19	9
10/17/81	12/12/81	Don't Stop Believin'	Journey	8	20
3/14/81	4/11/81	Don't Stop The Music	Yarbrough & Peoples	19	13
9/29/79	10/27/79	Don't Stop 'Til You Get Enough	Michael Jackson	7	20
3/20/82	6/12/82	Don't Talk To Strangers	Rick Springfield	6	24
3/4/89	3/25/89	Don't Tell Me Lies	Breathe	18	4
2/12/83	3/26/83	Don't Tell Me You Love Me	Night Ranger	16	15
8/12/89	9/16/89	Don't Wanna Lose You	Gloria Estefan	3	10
8/20/88	9/24/88	Don't Worry Be Happy	Bobby McFerrin	1	13
3/30/85	6/1/85	Don't You (Forget About Me)	Simple Minds	2	17
4/24/82	6/26/82	Don't You Want Me	Human League	1	25
11/14/87	12/19/87	Don't You Want Me	Jody Watley	14	7
8/15/81	8/29/81	Double Dutch Bus	Frankie Smith	26	9
5/20/89	7/1/89	Down Boys	Warrant	10	13
12/11/82	2/5/83	Down Under	Men At Work	2	22
9/2/89	10/21/89	Dr. Feelgood	Motley Crue	2	9

Debut	Peak	Title	Artist	Pos	Wks
9/5/81	9/26/81	Draw Of The Cards	Kim Carnes	23	9
10/13/79	12/8/79	Dream Police	Cheap Trick	8	19
11/29/80	12/6/80	Dreamer	Supertramp	35	8
11/24/79	12/15/79	Dreaming	Blondie	23	12
5/14/88	5/28/88	Dreaming	Orchestral Manoeuvres In The Dark	19	5
10/25/80	12/6/80	Dreaming	Cliff Richard	17	19
6/14/86	7/5/86	Dreams	Van Halen	28	7
8/2/86	10/4/86	Dreamtime	Daryl Hall	20	13
8/17/85	9/28/85	Dress You Up	Madonna	7	15
6/24/89	7/22/89	Dressed For Success	Roxette	9	7
8/4/84	9/1/84	Drive	Cars	12	18
2/25/89	3/18/89	Driven Out	Fixx	23	4
9/13/80	10/18/80	Drivin' My Life Away	Eddie Rabbitt	5	24
11/7/87	12/19/87	Dude (Looks Like A Lady)	Aerosmith	13	11
11/22/80	12/20/80	Dukes Of Hazzard (Good Ol' Boys), Theme From The	Waylon Jennings	17	18
9/1/84	9/29/84	Dynamite	Jermaine Jackson	12	12
12/3/88	12/24/88	Early In The Morning	Robert Palmer	21	4
12/22/84	2/2/85	Easy Lover	Philip Bailey with Phil Collins	1	18
3/17/84	4/14/84	Eat It	"Weird Al" Yankovic	3	14
4/17/82	5/22/82	Ebony And Ivory	Paul McCartney with Stevie Wonder	1	22
8/22/87	10/3/87	Edge Of A Broken Heart	Bon Jovi	10	12
7/5/86	8/2/86	Edge Of Heaven, The	Wham!	14	11
1/30/82	3/27/82	Edge Of Seventeen (Just Like The White Winged Dove)	Stevie Nicks	11	17
3/6/82	4/17/82	867-5309/Jenny	Tommy Tutone	5	23
7/22/89	9/9/89	18 And Life	Skid Row	3	14
10/26/85	12/21/85	Election Day	Arcadia	6	16
6/4/83	7/9/83	Electric Avenue	Eddy Grant	1	19
4/8/89	5/13/89	Electric Youth	Debbie Gibson	5	8
6/6/81	7/11/81	Elvira	Oak Ridge Boys	7	34
11/2/85	12/14/85	Emergency	Kool & the Gang	26	13
9/13/86	11/15/86	Emotion In Motion	Ric Ocasek	25	14
7/12/80	8/23/80	Emotional Rescue	Rolling Stones	3	19
7/22/89	8/26/89	End Of The Innocence, The	Don Henley	7	7
8/8/81	9/5/81	Endless Love	Diana Ross & Lionel Richie	1	27

Debut	Peak	Title	Artist	Pos	Wks
1/23/88	4/2/88	Endless Summer Nights	Richard Marx	1	15
1/27/90	3/17/90	Escapade	Janet Jackson	1	15
12/1/79	1/12/80	Escape (The Pina Colada Song)	Rupert Holmes	1	20
2/4/89	4/8/89	Eternal Flame	Bangles	1	16
2/9/80	3/15/80	Even It Up	Heart	21	15
3/19/83	4/30/83	Even Now	Bob Seger & the Silver Bullet Band	18	15
7/31/82	8/21/82	Even The Nights Are Better	Air Supply	10	14
2/13/88	3/5/88	Ever Since The World Began	Tommy Shaw	22	4
6/4/83	8/6/83	Every Breath You Take	Police	1	28
5/23/87	6/27/87	Every Little Kiss	Bruce Hornsby & the Range	26	7
4/22/89	5/20/89	Every Little Step	Bobby Brown	9	9
10/17/81	12/12/81	Every Little Thing She Does Is Magic	Police	6	24
10/29/88	12/24/88	Every Rose Has Its Thorn	Poison	1	18
8/10/85	9/28/85	Every Step Of The Way	John Waite	25	12
11/29/80	1/31/81	Every Woman In The World	Air Supply	10	18
1/11/86	2/8/86	Everybody Dance	Ta Mara & the Seen	26	9
10/25/86	12/27/86	Everybody Have Fun Tonight	Wang Chung	4	16
4/13/85	6/29/85	Everybody Wants To Rule The World	Tears For Fears	1	20
10/2/82	12/11/82	Everybody Wants You	Billy Squier	11	20
10/26/85	1/18/86	Everyday	James Taylor	46	13
3/4/89	4/22/89	Everyday Is Halloween	Ministry	15	10
12/9/89	1/13/90	Everything	Jody Watley	11	12
11/30/85	2/8/86	Everything In My Heart	Corey Hart	37	12
3/23/85	5/11/85	Everything She Wants	Wham!	11	19
10/11/86	11/1/86	Everytime You Cry	Outfield	47	4
5/25/85	7/20/85	Everytime You Go Away	Paul Young	14	19
7/9/83	8/20/83	Ewok Celebration	Meco	4	15
4/22/89	6/3/89	Excitable	Def Leppard	16	7
5/27/89	6/24/89	Express Yourself	Madonna	12	6
9/18/82	10/30/82	Eye In The Sky	Alan Parsons Project	3	18
6/12/82	7/3/82	Eye Of The Tiger	Survivor	1	23
6/9/84	7/14/84	Eyes Without A Face	Billy Idol	5	15
11/9/85	1/18/86	Face The Face	Pete Townshend	14	17

Debut	Peak	Title	Artist	Pos	Wks
1/24/87	2/28/87	Facts Of Love	Jeff Lorber featuring Karyn White	20	6
10/31/87	12/19/87	Faith	George Michael	1	17
4/23/83	6/11/83	Faithfully	Journey	19	18
8/27/88	10/8/88	Fallen Angel	Poison	8	9
11/29/86	1/17/87	Falling In Love (Uh-Oh)	Miami Sound Machine	21	9
8/30/80	9/27/80	Fame	Irene Cara	18	14
5/28/83	7/16/83	Family Man	Daryl Hall & John Oates	9	14
3/27/82	5/8/82	Fantasy	Aldo Nova	16	18
9/3/83	10/1/83	Far From Over	Frank Stallone	12	12
5/2/87	6/13/87	Fascinated	Company B	5	12
8/20/88	9/10/88	Fast Car	Tracy Chapman	2	6
2/6/88	3/12/88	Father Figure	George Michael	2	13
3/8/86	4/19/86	Feel It Again	Honeymoon Suite	37	9
9/17/83	10/22/83	Fight Fire With Fire	Kansas	26	8
1/24/87	3/7/87	(You Gotta) Fight For Your Right (To Party)	Beastie Boys	2	11
1/31/87	4/4/87	Final Countdown, The	Europe	9	11
3/20/82	4/24/82	Find Another Fool	Quarterflash	17	11
4/11/81	6/6/81	Find Your Way Back	Jefferson Starship	15	17
5/5/84	5/26/84	Fine Fine Day, A	Tony Carey	28	8
4/11/87	5/2/87	Finer Things, The	Steve Winwood	18	5
7/18/81	8/22/81	Fire And Ice	Pat Benatar	10	19
3/22/80	5/3/80	Fire Lake	Bob Seger	6	21
8/17/85	9/21/85	First Night	Survivor	44	7
6/18/88	7/23/88	Flame, The	Cheap Trick	1	13
5/7/83	5/28/83	Flashdance... What A Feeling	Irene Cara	1	29
9/24/83	10/29/83	Foolin'	Def Leppard	15	14
6/4/88	7/2/88	Foolish Beat	Debbie Gibson	2	11
12/16/89	12/16/89	Foolish Heart	Sharon Bryant	29	1
12/8/84	1/26/85	Foolish Heart	Steve Perry	33	14
11/1/86	11/29/86	Foolish Pride	Daryl Hall	41	6
2/11/84	4/7/84	Footloose	Kenny Loggins	1	25
3/29/86	4/26/86	For America	Jackson Browne	27	7
12/13/86	1/24/87	For Tonight	Nancy Martinez	17	8
4/18/81	5/30/81	For You	Manfred Mann's Earth Band	14	18
8/22/81	10/24/81	For Your Eyes Only	Sheena Easton	6	24
3/31/90	5/5/90	Forever	Kiss	11	6
7/6/85	8/3/85	Forever	Kenny Loggins	31	11

Debut	Peak	Title	Artist	Pos	Wks
4/20/85	5/4/85	Forever Man	Eric Clapton	25	7
11/19/88	12/10/88	Forever Young	Alphaville	17	4
8/27/88	10/1/88	Forever Young	Rod Stewart	16	7
4/1/89	5/13/89	Forever Your Girl	Paula Abdul	4	15
6/19/82	8/7/82	Forget Me Nots	Patrice Rushen	11	14
8/24/85	10/12/85	Fortress Around Your Heart	Sting	12	14
9/21/85	10/19/85	Four In The Morning (I Can't Take Any More)	Night Ranger	17	9
12/30/89	1/27/90	Free Fallin'	Tom Petty	2	19
7/20/85	8/24/85	Freedom	Wham!	23	15
9/27/86	10/18/86	Freedom Overspill	Steve Winwood	41	7
7/27/85	9/21/85	Freeway Of Love	Aretha Franklin	4	15
3/20/82	4/17/82	Freeze-Frame	J. Geils Band	3	20
12/13/86	1/17/87	French Kissin	Debbie Harry	22	9
5/4/85	6/1/85	Fresh	Kool & the Gang	12	12
8/26/89	9/2/89	Friends	Jody Watley with Eric B. & Rakim	16	3
8/9/86	9/20/86	Friends And Lovers	Gloria Loring & Carl Anderson	1	16
2/25/89	4/29/89	Funky Cold Medina	Tone Loc	2	16
5/9/87	7/18/87	Funky Town	Pseudo Echo	3	17
5/3/80	6/14/80	Funkytown	Lipps, Inc.	3	20
11/29/86	1/10/87	Future's So Bright, I Gotta Wear Shades, The	Timbuk 3	15	7
1/17/81	2/28/81	Games People Play	Alan Parsons Project	8	19
7/26/80	9/6/80	Games Without Frontiers	Peter Gabriel	5	18
6/27/81	8/8/81	Gemini Dream	Moody Blues	11	15
3/28/81	4/11/81	Generals And Majors	XTC	29	9
3/13/82	4/17/82	Genius Of Love	Tom Tom Club	18	14
10/30/82	11/20/82	Get Closer	Linda Ronstadt	22	11
5/1/82	6/19/82	Get Down On It	Kool & the Gang	14	19
6/8/85	7/27/85	Get It On (Bang A Gong)	Power Station	17	15
11/4/89	12/2/89	Get On Your Feet	Gloria Estefan	13	11
3/12/88	4/16/88	Get Outta My Dreams, Get Into My Car	Billy Ocean	1	16
3/28/87	4/18/87	Get That Love	Thompson Twins	28	5
2/24/90	4/21/90	Get Up (Before The Night Is Over)	Technotronic	1	11
6/22/85	7/13/85	Getcha Back	Beach Boys	32	8
7/7/84	8/4/84	Ghostbusters	Ray Parker, Jr.	1	23
4/23/83	5/21/83	Gimme All Your Lovin	ZZ Top	20	18

Debut	Peak	Title	Artist	Pos	Wks
6/28/80	8/9/80	Gimme Some Lovin'	Blues Brothers	3	18
8/30/86	10/4/86	Girl Can't Help It	Journey	42	9
8/19/89	9/16/89	Girl I'm Gonna Miss You	Milli Vanilli	1	15
11/27/82	12/25/82	Girl Is Mine, The	Michael Jackson & Paul McCartney	7	13
2/25/89	4/22/89	Girl You Know It's True	Milli Vanilli	1	12
2/27/88	4/23/88	Girlfriend	Pebbles	4	11
4/28/84	5/12/84	Girls	Dwight Twilley	30	7
5/23/87	7/25/87	Girls, Girls, Girls	Motley Crue	9	13
2/4/84	2/25/84	Girls Just Want To Have Fun	Cyndi Lauper	4	22
10/6/84	11/3/84	Girls With Guns	Tommy Shaw	30	9
4/5/80	4/19/80	Give It All You Got	Chuck Mangione	27	7
3/3/84	4/14/84	Give It Up	KC	7	15
9/6/80	9/20/80	Give Me The Night	George Benson	17	13
7/18/87	8/29/87	Give To Live	Sammy Hagar	16	8
2/14/81	3/14/81	Giving It Up For Your Love	Delbert McClinton	23	9
11/12/88	12/17/88	Giving You The Best That I Got	Anita Baker	5	10
8/25/84	10/13/84	Glamorous Life, The	Sheila E.	4	17
10/30/82	11/27/82	Gloria	Laura Branigan	1	27
6/1/85	7/20/85	Glory Days	Bruce Springsteen	8	17
6/7/86	8/2/86	Glory Of Love	Peter Cetera	2	20
11/23/85	1/18/86	Go Home	Stevie Wonder	25	14
9/8/84	10/13/84	Go Insane	Lindsey Buckingham	18	11
6/12/82	7/24/82	Going To A Go-Go	Rolling Stones	14	16
9/29/79	11/3/79	Good Girls Don't	Knack	7	18
11/8/86	11/22/86	Good Music	Joan Jett & the Blackhearts	47	6
4/22/89	7/1/89	Good Thing	Fine Young Cannibals	2	20
7/4/87	7/18/87	Good Times	INXS & Jimmy Barnes	34	5
11/30/85	1/25/86	Goodbye	Night Ranger	16	14
12/25/82	2/19/83	Goody Two Shoes	Adam Ant	5	18
5/18/85	6/15/85	Goonies 'R' Good Enough, The	Cyndi Lauper	23	14
2/18/84	3/24/84	Got A Hold On Me	Christine McVie	21	14
11/7/87	1/2/88	Got My Mind Set On You	George Harrison	1	19
12/20/80	2/14/81	Got To Rock On	Kansas	35	10
6/27/81	8/22/81	"Greatest American Hero" (Believe It Or Not), Theme From	Joey Scarbury	2	24
3/29/86	5/24/86	Greatest Love Of All	Whitney Houston	1	17

Debut	Peak	Title	Artist	Pos	Wks
9/17/88	10/29/88	Groovy Kind Of Love	Phil Collins	1	13
12/6/80	1/10/81	Guilty	Barbra Streisand & Barry Gibb	13	22
10/16/82	11/6/82	Gypsy	Fleetwood Mac	13	10
10/20/84	12/15/84	Had A Dream (Sleeping With The Enemy)	Roger Hodgson	16	15
12/8/79	12/29/79	Half The Way	Crystal Gayle	22	10
12/11/82	1/22/83	Hand To Hold On To	John Cougar	24	11
7/9/88	8/20/88	Hands To Heaven	Breathe	1	11
7/15/89	8/19/89	Hangin' Tough	New Kids On The Block	1	13
7/25/87	8/8/87	Happy	Surface	28	4
8/25/84	10/20/84	Hard Habit To Break	Chicago	6	21
9/12/81	10/24/81	Hard To Say	Dan Fogelberg	18	19
6/12/82	8/21/82	Hard To Say I'm Sorry/Getaway	Chicago	1	28
12/12/81	2/6/82	Harden My Heart	Quarterflash	3	21
3/15/86	4/12/86	Harlem Shuffle	Rolling Stones	5	13
11/28/87	1/30/88	Hazy Shade Of Winter	Bangles	2	16
1/17/81	2/28/81	He Can't Love You	Michael Stanley Band	9	16
12/1/79	1/12/80	Head Games	Foreigner	16	12
4/14/84	5/19/84	Head Over Heels	Go-Go's	19	13
9/14/85	10/19/85	Head Over Heels	Tears For Fears	11	14
4/11/87	6/20/87	Head To Toe	Lisa Lisa & Cult Jam	2	16
6/24/89	7/29/89	Headed For A Heartbreak	Winger	8	8
6/7/86	6/28/86	Headed For The Future	Neil Diamond	45	5
10/29/83	12/3/83	Heart And Soul	Huey Lewis & the News	13	20
6/6/87	8/8/87	Heart And Soul	T'Pau	6	19
10/9/82	11/6/82	Heart Attack	Olivia Newton-John	4	17
5/17/80	6/7/80	Heart Hotels	Dan Fogelberg	30	10
5/26/84	6/30/84	Heart Of Rock & Roll, The	Huey Lewis & the News	8	16
1/8/83	2/5/83	Heart To Heart	Kenny Loggins	19	15
9/29/79	11/17/79	Heartache Tonight	Eagles	4	22
8/30/86	10/11/86	Heartbeat	Don Johnson	16	12
4/4/87	5/23/87	Heartbreak Beat	Psychedelic Furs	11	9
3/8/80	4/12/80	Heartbreaker	Pat Benatar	6	20
11/27/82	1/8/83	Heartbreaker	Dionne Warwick	14	14
10/16/82	11/6/82	Heartlight	Neil Diamond	7	15
7/25/81	8/22/81	Hearts	Marty Balin	20	12
1/17/81	3/21/81	Hearts On Fire	Randy Meisner	15	16

Debut	Peak	Title	Artist	Pos	Wks
1/19/85	3/16/85	Heat Is On, The	Glenn Frey	1	22
5/1/82	6/19/82	Heat Of The Moment	Asia	6	24
4/18/87	5/23/87	Heat Of The Night	Bryan Adams	15	7
4/14/84	4/21/84	Heaven	Bryan Adams	46	2
4/20/85	6/22/85	Heaven	Bryan Adams	4	19
7/15/89	9/23/89	Heaven	Warrant	2	17
4/8/89	4/22/89	Heaven Help Me	Deon Estus with George Michael	16	5
8/16/86	10/11/86	Heaven In Your Eyes	Loverboy	29	12
9/26/87	11/28/87	Heaven Is a Place On Earth	Belinda Carlisle	1	22
10/3/81	10/24/81	Heavy Metal (Takin' A Ride)	Don Felder	22	11
2/8/86	2/22/86	He'll Never Love You (Like I Do)	Freddie Jackson	31	6
3/24/84	5/5/84	Hello	Lionel Richie	1	22
11/24/84	12/15/84	Hello Again	Cars	29	9
2/28/81	4/11/81	Hello Again	Neil Diamond	12	13
3/21/81	5/2/81	Her Town Too	James Taylor & J.D. Souther	20	15
3/3/90	4/14/90	Here And Now	Luther Vandross	4	10
2/25/84	3/17/84	Here Comes The Rain Again	Eurythmics	10	16
11/7/81	12/19/81	Here I Am (Just When I Thought I Was Over You)	Air Supply	7	15
7/25/87	9/19/87	Here I Go Again	Whitesnake	1	19
1/27/90	3/3/90	Here We Are	Gloria Estefan	14	11
8/1/87	9/5/87	He's My Girl	David Hallyday	35	9
10/25/80	12/13/80	He's So Shy	Pointer Sisters	5	18
8/5/89	8/26/89	Hey Ladies	Beastie Boys	12	7
12/27/80	2/14/81	Hey Nineteen	Steely Dan	11	18
1/17/87	1/31/87	Hey Rocky	Boris Badenough	35	3
8/25/84	9/15/84	High On Emotion	Chris DeBurgh	27	7
1/26/85	3/16/85	High On You	Survivor	24	15
6/14/86	8/16/86	Higher Love	Steve Winwood	7	21
3/8/80	4/12/80	Him	Rupert Holmes	8	15
10/11/86	11/29/86	Hip To Be Square	Huey Lewis & the News	16	14
10/8/88	11/12/88	Hippy Hippy Shake	Georgia Satellites	19	7
11/8/80	1/17/81	Hit Me With Your Best Shot	Pat Benatar	2	29
7/3/82	8/14/82	Hold Me	Fleetwood Mac	5	19
3/24/84	5/5/84	Hold Me Now	Thompson Twins	5	17

Debut	Peak	Title	Artist	Pos	Wks
10/11/80	11/8/80	Hold On	Kansas	18	16
10/2/82	10/16/82	Hold On	Santana	17	11
4/4/81	6/13/81	Hold On Loosely	.38 Special	5	22
9/5/81	9/26/81	Hold On Tight	Electric Light Orchestra	19	13
5/21/88	7/30/88	Hold On To The Nights	Richard Marx	3	15
5/24/86	7/19/86	Holding Back The Years	Simply Red	1	15
12/24/88	1/14/89	Holding On	Steve Winwood	18	5
2/11/84	2/25/84	Holiday	Madonna	18	11
7/25/87	9/12/87	Holiday	Other Ones	18	10
3/6/82	4/17/82	Hollywood	Shooting Star	32	12
11/21/87	1/30/88	Honestly	Stryper	4	16
1/9/82	2/20/82	Hooked On Classics	Royal Philharmonic Orchestra	12	18
12/15/84	1/5/85	Hot For Teacher	Van Halen	33	6
6/18/83	7/30/83	Hot Girls In Love	Loverboy	16	17
10/4/80	10/25/80	Hot Rod Hearts	Robbie Dupree	31	8
9/19/87	10/31/87	Hourglass	Squeeze	20	8
9/17/83	10/22/83	How Am I Supposed To Live Without You	Laura Branigan	15	13
12/30/89	2/3/90	How Am I Supposed To Live Without You	Michael Bolton	1	18
10/8/88	11/12/88	How Can I Fall	Breathe	13	10
4/7/90	5/5/90	How Can We Be Lovers	Michael Bolton	4	5
3/15/80	4/19/80	How Do I Make You	Linda Ronstadt	16	14
12/14/85	3/1/86	How Will I Know	Whitney Houston	1	22
9/27/86	11/15/86	Human	Human League	2	17
8/20/83	9/10/83	Human Nature	Michael Jackson	21	13
9/24/83	10/22/83	Human Touch	Rick Springfield	27	8
1/9/88	2/20/88	Hungry Eyes	Eric Carmen	2	14
11/1/80	12/20/80	Hungry Heart	Bruce Springsteen	5	21
2/5/83	3/5/83	Hungry Like The Wolf	Duran Duran	2	20
5/3/80	5/31/80	Hurt So Bad	Linda Ronstadt	13	14
5/29/82	7/24/82	Hurts So Good	John Cougar	2	25
2/20/88	3/19/88	Hysteria	Def Leppard	16	7
9/20/86	11/15/86	I Am By Your Side	Corey Hart	34	11
2/4/89	3/18/89	I Beg Your Pardon	Kon Kan	6	10
6/16/84	8/25/84	I Can Dream About You	Dan Hartman	5	18
2/7/87	3/7/87	I Can Take Care Of Myself	Billy Vera & the Beaters	28	5
11/10/84	12/8/84	I Can't Drive 55	Sammy Hagar	21	10

Debut	Peak	Title	Artist	Pos	Wks
12/19/81	1/30/82	I Can't Go For That (No Can Do)	Daryl Hall & John Oates	2	20
5/17/80	6/7/80	I Can't Help It	Andy Gibb & Olivia Newton-John	27	7
10/6/84	12/15/84	I Can't Hold Back	Survivor	22	22
7/26/80	9/13/80	I Can't Let Go	Linda Ronstadt	31	10
3/28/81	5/2/81	I Can't Stand It	Eric Clapton	15	13
3/1/80	5/3/80	I Can't Tell You Why	Eagles	11	20
2/22/86	3/22/86	I Can't Wait	Stevie Nicks	30	8
4/26/86	6/7/86	I Can't Wait	Nu Shooz	4	15
11/21/87	1/23/88	I Could Never Take The Place Of Your Man	Prince	10	11
8/16/86	11/8/86	I Didn't Mean To Turn You On	Robert Palmer	3	19
1/15/83	1/29/83	I Do	J. Geils Band	29	9
10/31/87	12/5/87	I Do You	Jets	21	6
2/12/83	3/19/83	I Don't Care Anymore	Phil Collins	24	12
7/4/81	8/15/81	I Don't Need You	Kenny Rogers	7	17
7/9/88	8/13/88	I Don't Wanna Go On With You Like That	Elton John	9	7
7/2/88	8/27/88	I Don't Wanna Live Without Your Love	Chicago	5	11
9/3/88	9/17/88	I Don't Want To Be A Hero	Johnny Hates Jazz	20	3
10/15/88	11/26/88	I Don't Want Your Love	Duran Duran	8	9
10/20/84	12/1/84	I Do'wanna Know	REO Speedwagon	35	10
9/29/84	12/8/84	I Feel For You	Chaka Khan	1	23
9/23/89	10/21/89	I Feel The Earth Move	Martika	12	5
2/6/88	3/19/88	I Get Weak	Belinda Carlisle	5	12
3/14/87	4/18/87	I Go Crazy	Flesh For Lulu	19	6
1/20/90	3/3/90	I Go To Extremes	Billy Joel	12	12
8/31/85	10/12/85	I Got You Babe	UB40 with Chrissie Hynde	14	11
1/15/83	1/29/83	I Gotta Try	Michael McDonald	40	4
1/7/84	2/4/84	I Guess That's Why They Call It The Blues	Elton John	3	14
9/3/88	10/1/88	I Hate Myself For Loving You	Joan Jett & the Blackhearts	3	8
9/5/87	10/10/87	I Heard A Rumour	Bananarama	7	13
9/15/84	10/6/84	I Just Called To Say I Love You	Stevie Wonder	1	20
8/15/87	9/19/87	I Just Can't Stop Loving You	Michael Jackson	3	15
8/28/82	10/16/82	I Keep Forgettin' (Every Time You're Near)	Michael McDonald	7	17

Debut	Peak	Title	Artist	Pos	Wks
10/26/85	11/30/85	I Knew The Bride (When She Use To Rock And Roll)	Nick Lowe & his Cowboy Outfit	21	12
3/7/87	4/25/87	I Knew You Were Waiting (For Me)	Aretha Franklin & George Michael	3	15
3/12/83	4/16/83	I Know There's Something Going On	Frida	7	14
4/4/87	5/16/87	I Know What I Like	Huey Lewis & the News	20	9
7/15/89	8/19/89	I Like It	Dino	4	11
11/18/89	12/9/89	I Live By The Groove	Paul Carrack	17	5
12/12/87	2/6/88	I Live For Your Love	Natalie Cole	7	10
1/17/81	3/7/81	I Love A Rainy Night	Eddie Rabbitt	4	19
2/6/82	3/13/82	I Love Rock 'N Roll	Joan Jett & the Blackhearts	1	28
5/23/81	7/4/81	I Love You	Climax Blues Band	3	18
11/29/80	1/10/81	I Made It Through The Rain	Barry Manilow	20	15
11/23/85	12/28/85	I Miss You	Klymaxx	4	18
4/25/81	5/16/81	I Missed Again	Phil Collins	10	15
8/15/87	9/19/87	I Need Love	L.L. Cool J	14	7
5/13/89	5/20/89	I Only Wanna Be With You	Samantha Fox	21	2
9/18/82	10/30/82	I Ran (So Far Away)	Flock Of Seagulls	5	18
12/10/88	1/28/89	I Remember Holding You	Boys Club	11	8
10/28/89	1/13/90	I Remember You	Skid Row	2	26
3/19/88	4/23/88	I Saw Him Standing There	Tiffany	3	9
7/2/88	7/16/88	I Should Be So Lucky	Kylie Minogue	21	5
6/25/88	7/23/88	I Still Believe	Brenda K. Starr	10	8
1/7/84	2/11/84	I Still Can't Get Over Loving You	Ray Parker, Jr.	13	18
6/13/87	8/15/87	I Still Haven't Found What I'm Looking For	U2	3	17
3/1/86	4/19/86	I Think It's Love	Jermaine Jackson	26	13
8/15/87	10/31/87	I Think We're Alone Now	Tiffany	1	21
5/24/86	6/21/86	I Wanna Be A Cowboy	Boys Don't Cry	4	11
4/14/90	5/5/90	I Wanna Be Rich	Calloway	7	4
2/9/80	3/1/80	I Wanna Be Your Lover	Prince	21	8
5/16/87	6/27/87	I Wanna Dance With Somebody (Who Loves Me)	Whitney Houston	1	18
1/10/87	2/7/87	I Wanna Go Back	Eddie Money	30	5
12/3/88	1/21/89	I Wanna Have Some Fun	Samantha Fox	2	12
2/18/84	3/24/84	I Want A New Drug	Huey Lewis & the News	6	18
6/6/87	7/18/87	I Want Action	Poison	23	9
2/27/88	4/9/88	I Want Her	Keith Sweat	6	8

Debut	Peak	Title	Artist	Pos	Wks
12/12/87	2/13/88	I Want To Be Your Man	Roger	3	13
12/22/84	2/9/85	I Want To Know What Love Is	Foreigner	3	20
5/30/87	8/1/87	I Want Your Sex	George Michael	1	23
3/14/87	4/11/87	I Will Be There	Glass Tiger	26	5
2/3/90	3/17/90	I Wish It Would Rain Down	Phil Collins	5	14
9/5/87	9/5/87	I Won't Forget You	Poison	43	1
4/2/83	5/14/83	I Won't Hold You Back	Toto	15	16
12/8/84	1/19/85	I Would Die 4 U	Prince & the Revolution	5	15
7/4/87	8/8/87	I'd Still Say Yes	Klymaxx	10	8
7/5/86	8/9/86	If Anybody Had A Heart	John Waite	39	6
10/15/83	11/12/83	If Anyone Falls	Stevie Nicks	20	13
7/28/84	9/8/84	If Ever You're In My Arms Again	Peabo Bryson	9	14
9/9/89	10/14/89	If I Could Turn Back Time	Cher	1	11
1/7/84	2/4/84	If I'd Been The One	.38 Special	27	11
8/20/88	9/24/88	If It Isn't Love	New Edition	6	9
6/14/86	7/5/86	If She Knew What She Wants	Bangles	30	7
5/2/87	5/23/87	If She Would Have Been Faithful	Chicago	35	4
8/11/84	9/8/84	If This Is It	Huey Lewis & the News	10	12
6/3/89	7/15/89	If You Don't Know Me By Now	Simply Red	2	13
11/5/88	11/26/88	If You Feel It	Denise Lopez	24	5
3/29/86	5/24/86	If You Leave	Orchestral Manoeuvres In The Dark	9	15
6/22/85	8/3/85	If You Love Somebody Set Them Free	Sting	5	16
6/5/82	7/31/82	If You Want My Love	Cheap Trick	23	15
10/23/82	11/13/82	I.G.Y. (What A Beautiful World)	Donald Fagen	14	14
1/28/89	3/4/89	Iko Iko	Belle Stars	7	9
9/17/88	10/29/88	I'll Always Love You	Taylor Dayne	6	9
12/27/86	3/21/87	I'll Be Alright Without You	Journey	30	7
4/15/89	6/10/89	I'll Be Loving You (Forever)	New Kids On The Block	7	15
8/30/86	11/29/86	I'll Be Over You	Toto	25	18
3/11/89	5/6/89	I'll Be There For You	Bon Jovi	4	11
4/15/89	5/6/89	I'll Be You	Replacements	15	5
1/30/82	3/6/82	I'll Fall In Love Again	Sammy Hagar	30	12
8/13/83	9/17/83	I'll Tumble 4 Ya	Culture Club	13	13
4/21/84	6/2/84	I'll Wait	Van Halen	24	14
7/5/80	8/9/80	I'm Alive	Electric Light Orchestra	25	17

Debut	Peak	Title	Artist	Pos	Wks
9/20/80	11/8/80	I'm Alright	Kenny Loggins	3	20
7/7/84	7/21/84	I'm Free (Heaven Helps The Man)	Kenny Loggins	27	8
9/7/85	10/5/85	I'm Goin' Down	Bruce Springsteen	9	11
9/14/85	10/26/85	I'm Gonna Tear Your Playhouse Down	Paul Young	19	11
3/1/86	3/29/86	I'm Not The One	Cars	43	5
3/2/85	4/6/85	I'm On Fire	Bruce Springsteen	8	18
9/8/84	10/20/84	I'm So Excited	Pointer Sisters	2	20
6/18/83	7/9/83	I'm Still Standing	Elton John	17	15
6/10/89	7/15/89	I'm That Type Of Guy	L.L. Cool J	5	7
11/30/85	2/1/86	I'm Your Man	Wham!	9	17
11/19/83	12/17/83	In A Big Country	Big Country	13	14
7/12/80	8/23/80	In America	Charlie Daniels Band	8	19
9/19/87	10/31/87	In My Dreams	REO Speedwagon	17	9
5/4/85	6/15/85	In My House	Mary Jane Girls	10	14
5/30/81	7/4/81	In The Air Tonight	Phil Collins	4	17
9/5/81	10/31/81	In The Dark	Billy Squier	10	17
5/24/86	6/28/86	In The Shape Of A Heart	Jackson Browne	42	7
4/25/87	6/13/87	In Too Deep	Genesis	8	13
9/13/86	10/4/86	In Your Eyes	Peter Gabriel	26	10
5/20/89	7/8/89	In Your Eyes	Peter Gabriel	3	14
11/5/88	1/7/89	In Your Room	Bangles	5	11
6/30/84	7/21/84	Infatuation	Rod Stewart	14	12
5/10/86	6/21/86	Innocent Eyes	Graham Nash	41	7
6/8/85	7/6/85	Into The Groove	Madonna	3	15
6/22/85	8/10/85	Invincible (Theme From The Legend Of Billie Jean)	Pat Benatar	23	15
5/31/86	7/5/86	Invisible Touch	Genesis	5	16
3/29/86	5/31/86	Is It Love	Mr. Mister	26	13
6/25/83	8/27/83	Is There Something I Should Know	Duran Duran	18	16
11/1/86	12/27/86	Is This Love	Survivor	36	11
11/21/87	1/9/88	Is This Love	Whitesnake	4	12
9/24/83	11/12/83	Islands In The Stream	Kenny Rogers with Dolly Parton	1	22
10/27/84	12/8/84	It Ain't Enough	Corey Hart	27	12
9/3/88	9/24/88	It Would Take A Strong Strong Man	Rick Astley	11	6
5/26/84	6/23/84	It's A Miracle	Culture Club	20	9
7/9/83	8/6/83	It's A Mistake	Men At Work	17	14

Debut	Peak	Title	Artist	Pos	Wks
9/5/87	10/31/87	It's A Sin	Pet Shop Boys	5	13
5/3/80	5/24/80	It's Hard To Be Humble	Mac Davis	15	18
7/30/83	8/20/83	It's Inevitable	Charlie	34	8
12/27/80	1/31/81	It's My Turn	Diana Ross	23	12
8/8/87	8/29/87	It's Not Over ('Til It's Over)	Starship	30	5
11/29/86	12/20/86	It's Not You, It's Not Me	KBC Band	47	4
12/21/85	1/25/86	It's Only Love	Bryan Adams & Tina Turner	28	8
10/30/82	12/4/82	It's Raining Again	Supertramp	10	17
5/31/80	7/26/80	It's Still Rock And Roll To Me	Billy Joel	1	24
8/16/86	9/13/86	It's You	Bob Seger & the Silver Bullet Band	39	7
9/5/87	11/21/87	I've Been In Love Before	Cutting Crew	10	13
10/10/81	11/28/81	I've Done Everything For You	Rick Springfield	7	18
3/12/83	4/2/83	I've Got A Rock N' Roll Heart	Eric Clapton	15	14
4/14/84	4/21/84	I've Got You	Kind	31	6
5/8/82	6/5/82	I've Never Been To Me	Charlene	6	14
7/31/82	9/25/82	Jack & Diane	John Cougar	1	21
8/6/88	8/20/88	Jackie	Blue Zone U.K.	28	3
12/20/86	3/14/87	Jacob's Ladder	Huey Lewis & the News	7	15
12/22/84	1/26/85	Jamie	Ray Parker, Jr.	22	11
4/18/87	6/13/87	Jammin' Me	Tom Petty & the Heartbreakers	21	11
12/8/79	1/19/80	Jane	Jefferson Starship	6	16
1/20/90	2/24/90	Janie's Got A Gun	Aerosmith	2	13
3/26/83	5/7/83	Jeopardy	Greg Kihn Band	4	19
10/4/80	11/29/80	Jesse	Carly Simon	5	19
6/20/81	8/1/81	Jessie's Girl	Rick Springfield	1	27
1/14/84	2/25/84	Joanna	Kool & the Gang	5	18
8/19/89	9/23/89	Joy And Pain	Rob Base & D.J. E-Z Rock	9	10
3/6/82	4/3/82	Juke Box Hero	Foreigner	14	11
1/21/84	3/3/84	Jump	Van Halen	2	25
5/19/84	7/14/84	Jump (For My Love)	Pointer Sisters	7	18
9/12/87	10/17/87	Jump Start	Natalie Cole	11	7
9/27/86	11/8/86	Jumpin' Jack Flash	Aretha Franklin	10	12
2/9/85	3/16/85	Jungle Love	Time	6	14
4/27/85	5/25/85	Just A Gigolo/I Ain't Got Nobody	David Lee Roth	12	12
2/9/85	3/23/85	Just Another Night	Mick Jagger	19	13

Debut	Peak	Title	Artist	Pos	Wks
7/20/85	8/3/85	Just As I Am	Air Supply	32	7
3/25/89	4/8/89	Just Because	Anita Baker	22	4
3/7/81	4/18/81	Just Between You And Me	April Wine	9	19
11/25/89	2/10/90	Just Between You And Me	Lou Gramm	3	19
6/25/88	7/23/88	Just Got Paid	Johnny Kemp	6	10
12/12/87	1/9/88	Just Like Heaven	Cure	21	6
1/23/88	3/5/88	Just Like Paradise	David Lee Roth	5	10
3/28/81	5/16/81	Just The Two Of Us	Grover Washington, Jr. & Bill Withers	8	17
4/18/87	6/13/87	Just To See Her	Smokey Robinson	12	11
12/24/83	2/4/84	Karma Chameleon	Culture Club	1	20
11/22/80	2/7/81	Keep On Loving You	REO Speedwagon	1	30
9/2/89	9/16/89	Keep On Movin'	Soul II Soul	14	5
6/12/82	8/7/82	Keep The Fire Burnin'	REO Speedwagon	13	17
11/15/86	2/7/87	Keep Your Hands To Yourself	Georgia Satellites	1	19
2/2/85	3/16/85	Keeping The Faith	Billy Joel	26	15
4/3/82	5/15/82	Key Largo	Bertie Higgins	4	17
6/21/86	7/12/86	Kind Of Magic, A	Queen	37	6
1/18/86	2/15/86	King For A Day	Thompson Twins	15	13
9/3/83	10/15/83	King Of Pain	Police	9	18
11/26/88	12/24/88	Kiss	Art Of Noise featuring Tom Jones	15	5
2/22/86	4/19/86	Kiss	Prince & the Revolution	1	18
5/16/87	7/25/87	Kiss Him Goodbye	Nylons	11	12
4/2/88	6/4/88	Kiss Me Deadly	Lita Ford	3	17
3/21/81	5/9/81	Kiss On My List	Daryl Hall & John Oates	3	19
10/1/88	11/5/88	Kokomo	Beach Boys	1	16
12/21/85	3/15/86	Kyrie	Mr. Mister	2	19
7/11/87	9/5/87	La Bamba	Los Lobos	1	21
3/7/87	5/16/87	La Isla Bonita	Madonna	3	17
10/27/79	12/1/79	Ladies Night	Kool & the Gang	8	25
10/18/80	12/6/80	Lady	Kenny Rogers	1	25
3/28/87	5/30/87	Lady In Red, The	Chris DeBurgh	2	18
11/1/86	1/31/87	Land Of Confusion	Genesis	8	16
7/5/80	7/26/80	Landlord	Gladys Knight & the Pips	34	8
2/25/84	3/24/84	Language Of Love, The	Dan Fogelberg	18	11
2/25/89	3/18/89	Last Mile, The	Cinderella	27	4

Debut	Peak	Title	Artist	Pos	Wks
4/15/89	4/15/89	Last Night	Traveling Wilburys	29	2
11/18/89	12/16/89	Last Worthless Evening, The	Don Henley	14	7
8/9/80	9/20/80	Late In The Evening	Paul Simon	12	18
8/6/83	9/17/83	Lawyers In Love	Jackson Browne	12	14
6/10/89	8/12/89	Lay Your Hands On Me	Bon Jovi	4	12
9/28/85	11/16/85	Lay Your Hands On Me	Thompson Twins	11	17
9/15/84	9/29/84	Layin' It On The Line	Jefferson Starship	38	5
2/6/82	3/6/82	Leader Of The Band	Dan Fogelberg	15	15
1/24/87	3/21/87	Lean On Me	Club Nouveau	1	18
10/31/81	12/12/81	Leather And Lace	Stevie Nicks with Don Henley	11	19
10/14/89	11/18/89	Leave A Light On	Belinda Carlisle	10	12
8/11/84	8/25/84	Leave A Tender Moment Alone	Billy Joel	31	10
8/23/80	9/27/80	Legend Of Wooley Swamp, The	Charlie Daniels Band	10	19
6/16/84	7/14/84	Legs	ZZ Top	8	15
5/9/87	6/27/87	Lessons In Love	Level 42	14	10
7/10/82	8/21/82	Let It Whip	Dazz Band	7	16
5/10/80	5/24/80	Let Me Be The Clock	Smokey Robinson	30	8
8/22/87	10/17/87	Let Me Be The One	Expose	17	13
6/21/80	7/19/80	Let Me Love You Tonight	Pure Prairie League	20	13
7/19/80	9/13/80	Let My Love Open The Door	Pete Townshend	9	17
11/26/83	2/4/84	Let The Music Play	Shannon	6	24
4/9/83	5/14/83	Let's Dance	David Bowie	2	25
1/16/82	2/20/82	Let's Get It Up	AC/DC	16	11
5/31/80	7/5/80	Let's Get Serious	Jermaine Jackson	19	13
2/14/87	4/25/87	Let's Go	Wang Chung	4	12
3/15/86	5/3/86	Let's Go All The Way	Sly Fox	9	14
8/25/84	9/22/84	Let's Go Crazy	Prince & the Revolution	3	25
12/19/81	1/30/82	Let's Groove	Earth, Wind & Fire	9	15
4/21/84	6/2/84	Let's Hear It For The Boy	Deniece Williams	1	17
2/14/87	3/21/87	Let's Wait Awhile	Janet Jackson	4	9
12/14/85	2/8/86	Life In A Northern Town	Dream Academy	9	17
7/20/85	8/24/85	Life In One Day	Howard Jones	22	10
5/30/81	7/11/81	Life Of Illusion, A	Joe Walsh	17	15
2/21/87	3/28/87	Light Of Day	Barbusters (Joan Jett & the Blackhearts)	23	7
8/11/84	9/1/84	Lights Out	Peter Wolf	20	11
3/25/89	4/29/89	Like A Prayer	Madonna	1	15

Debut	Peak	Title	Artist	Pos	Wks
5/24/86	6/28/86	Like A Rock	Bob Seger & the Silver Bullet Band	21	10
11/24/84	1/5/85	Like A Virgin	Madonna	1	19
11/8/86	11/15/86	Like Flames	Berlin	49	2
5/10/86	6/28/86	Like No Other Night	.38 Special	32	11
10/28/89	11/4/89	Listen To Your Heart	Roxette	17	6
6/29/85	7/13/85	Little By Little	Robert Plant	25	6
2/21/81	3/21/81	Little In Love, A	Cliff Richard	21	12
6/7/80	7/19/80	Little Jeannie	Elton John	8	17
12/24/88	1/21/89	Little Liar	Joan Jett & the Blackhearts	17	5
8/29/87	10/31/87	Little Lies	Fleetwood Mac	7	14
5/14/83	6/25/83	Little Red Corvette	Prince	4	18
1/7/89	2/18/89	Little Respect, A	Erasure	5	10
6/18/88	6/25/88	Little Walter	Tony! Toni! Tone!	29	2
11/1/86	12/6/86	(Forever) Live And Die	Orchestral Manoeuvres In The Dark	26	9
7/20/85	8/10/85	Live Every Moment	REO Speedwagon	46	8
4/19/86	6/14/86	Live To Tell	Madonna	2	16
2/6/82	3/6/82	Livin' In The Limelight	Peter Cetera	29	9
12/13/86	2/21/87	Livin' On A Prayer	Bon Jovi	1	18
7/4/87	8/15/87	Living In A Box	Living In a Box	29	7
1/24/81	3/21/81	Living In A Fantasy	Leo Sayer	32	13
12/21/85	2/15/86	Living In America	James Brown	7	18
11/4/89	11/25/89	Living In Sin	Bon Jovi	17	10
5/2/81	5/30/81	Living Inside Myself	Gino Vannelli	13	15
8/13/83	9/10/83	Living On The Edge	Jim Capaldi	31	13
2/11/89	3/25/89	Living Years, The	Mike + the Mechanics	1	14
8/20/88	10/22/88	Loco-Motion, The	Kylie Minogue	3	15
2/20/82	4/3/82	Lonely Nights	Bryan Adams	33	15
8/17/85	10/12/85	Lonely Ol' Night	John Cougar Mellencamp	9	17
1/19/85	2/2/85	Lonely School	Tommy Shaw	41	6
8/25/79	10/27/79	Lonesome Loser	Little River Band	6	21
12/15/79	2/2/80	Long Run, The	Eagles	14	14
1/26/80	3/15/80	Longer	Dan Fogelberg	3	19
5/12/84	6/16/84	Longest Time, The	Billy Joel	6	15
2/18/89	4/8/89	Look, The	Roxette	4	12
10/8/88	12/10/88	Look Away	Chicago	2	13
11/13/82	12/18/82	Look Of Love (Part One), The	ABC	10	19
10/4/80	11/15/80	Look What You've Done To Me	Boz Scaggs	9	13

Debut	Peak	Title	Artist	Pos	Wks
9/13/80	10/18/80	Lookin' For Love	Johnny Lee	6	16
3/7/87	5/9/87	Looking For A New Love	Jody Watley	1	19
2/25/84	3/31/84	Looks That Kill	Motley Crue	14	13
8/29/87	9/26/87	Lost In Emotion	Lisa Lisa & Cult Jam	16	10
4/5/80	6/7/80	Lost In Love	Air Supply	1	34
1/28/89	3/18/89	Lost In Your Eyes	Debbie Gibson	1	14
9/3/88	10/8/88	Love Bites	Def Leppard	1	13
2/8/86	3/1/86	Love Bizarre, A	Sheila E.	12	10
8/6/88	8/13/88	Love Changes (Everything)	Climie Fisher	25	2
4/28/90	5/5/90	Love Child	Sweet Sensation	24	2
1/24/87	2/14/87	Love For Sale	Talking Heads	27	4
9/16/89	10/21/89	Love In An Elevator	Aerosmith	11	7
12/18/82	1/15/83	Love In Store	Fleetwood Mac	31	9
10/22/83	12/3/83	Love Is A Battlefield	Pat Benatar	8	17
9/12/87	10/10/87	Love Is Contagious	Taja Sevelle	26	6
8/14/82	9/11/82	Love Is In Control (Finger On The Trigger)	Donna Summer	11	13
12/26/81	2/20/82	Love Is Like A Rock	Donnie Iris	5	17
8/19/89	9/2/89	Love Is The Drug	Roxy Music	21	5
11/9/85	12/14/85	Love Is The Seventh Wave	Sting	20	12
1/5/85	1/26/85	Love Light In Flight	Stevie Wonder	34	7
2/21/87	3/14/87	Love Like A Rocket	Bob Geldof	32	5
2/17/90	3/10/90	Love Me For Life	Stevie B	11	9
10/9/82	11/13/82	Love Me Tomorrow	Chicago	15	16
7/12/86	8/23/86	Love Of A Lifetime	Chaka Khan	32	7
8/8/81	9/12/81	Love On A Two Way Street	Stacy Lattisaw	19	11
11/1/80	1/10/81	Love On The Rocks	Neil Diamond	8	22
5/3/86	5/17/86	Love Parade, The	Dream Academy	40	6
7/25/87	9/5/87	Love Power	Dionne Warwick & Jeffrey Osborne	13	9
8/26/89	11/11/89	Love Shack	B-52's	5	25
4/7/84	5/12/84	Love Somebody	Rick Springfield	14	12
9/9/89	10/28/89	Love Song	Cure	2	14
5/24/80	7/5/80	Love Stinks	J. Geils Band	15	13
7/19/80	8/16/80	Love The World Away	Kenny Rogers	14	12
5/31/86	8/9/86	Love Touch	Rod Stewart	10	16
10/4/86	12/13/86	Love Will Conquer All	Lionel Richie	17	15
3/31/90	4/28/90	Love Will Lead You Back	Taylor Dayne	7	6
7/23/88	8/20/88	Love Will Save The Day	Whitney Houston	14	5

Debut	Peak	Title	Artist	Pos	Wks
9/4/82	10/2/82	Love Will Turn You Around	Kenny Rogers	21	11
1/10/87	2/28/87	Love You Down	Ready For The World	2	11
5/16/81	6/6/81	Love You Like I Never Loved Before	John O'Banion	38	6
9/6/86	10/11/86	Love Zone	Billy Ocean	18	8
8/14/82	10/2/82	Loved By You	Kind	15	20
11/29/80	12/6/80	Lovely One	Jacksons	33	8
1/12/85	2/16/85	Loverboy	Billy Ocean	4	15
3/2/85	4/6/85	Lovergirl	Teena Marie	10	13
6/19/82	8/14/82	Love's Been A Little Bit Hard On Me	Juice Newton	16	18
5/14/83	6/11/83	Love's Got A Line On You	Scandal	20	13
9/22/79	11/10/79	Lovin', Touchin', Squeezin'	Journey	2	25
9/8/84	9/29/84	Lucky One, The	Laura Branigan	28	9
9/15/84	10/20/84	Lucky Star	Madonna	7	14
6/20/87	8/15/87	Luka	Suzanne Vega	2	18
2/8/86	3/29/86	Lying	Peter Frampton	46	8
7/5/86	8/16/86	Mad About You	Belinda Carlisle	4	14
6/16/84	7/28/84	Magic	Cars	18	13
7/5/80	8/23/80	Magic	Olivia Newton-John	1	23
10/24/81	12/12/81	Magic Power	Triumph	14	15
12/3/83	1/7/84	Major Tom (Coming Home)	Peter Schilling	6	14
4/3/82	5/8/82	Make A Move On Me	Olivia Newton-John	12	13
8/14/82	10/16/82	Make Believe	Toto	25	12
5/14/88	7/2/88	Make It Real	Jets	5	12
7/30/88	9/3/88	Make Me Lose Control	Eric Carmen	5	8
5/29/82	6/19/82	Making Love	Roberta Flack	20	11
9/17/83	10/22/83	Making Love Out Of Nothing At All	Air Supply	2	20
3/5/88	4/9/88	Man In The Mirror	Michael Jackson	1	11
3/27/82	5/8/82	Man On The Corner	Genesis	23	15
7/5/86	8/30/86	Man Size Love	Klymaxx	14	14
2/28/87	3/28/87	Mandolin Rain	Bruce Hornsby & the Range	14	7
11/13/82	1/8/83	Maneater	Daryl Hall & John Oates	2	21
7/23/83	8/27/83	Maniac	Michael Sembello	4	18
3/1/86	4/19/86	Manic Monday	Bangles	8	15
7/18/87	8/29/87	Mary's Prayer	Danny Wilson	8	11
10/11/80	11/29/80	Master Blaster (Jammin')	Stevie Wonder	9	18
2/16/85	3/30/85	Material Girl	Madonna	2	18

Debut	Peak	Title	Artist	Pos	Wks
8/9/86	10/11/86	Matter Of Trust, A	Billy Joel	34	14
4/11/87	6/20/87	Meet Me Half Way	Kenny Loggins	22	12
6/4/88	7/30/88	Mercedes Boy	Pebbles	2	13
12/22/84	2/2/85	Method Of Modern Love	Daryl Hall & John Oates	15	17
9/21/85	10/26/85	Miami Vice Theme	Jan Hammer	1	20
11/20/82	12/11/82	Mickey	Toni Basil	1	23
2/4/84	2/25/84	Middle Of The Road	Pretenders	14	13
3/8/86	3/22/86	(How To Be A) Millionaire	ABC	33	5
3/2/85	3/30/85	Misled	Kool & the Gang	14	12
3/10/84	5/5/84	Miss Me Blind	Culture Club	9	16
7/8/89	7/29/89	Miss You Like Crazy	Natalie Cole	14	5
9/2/89	10/21/89	Miss You Much	Janet Jackson	1	16
3/9/85	4/13/85	Missing You	Diana Ross	5	14
7/21/84	9/15/84	Missing You	John Waite	3	20
7/26/86	9/20/86	Missionary Man	Eurythmics	13	13
6/21/80	8/2/80	Misunderstanding	Genesis	4	19
9/2/89	9/30/89	Mixed Emotions	Rolling Stones	6	6
6/23/84	7/7/84	Modern Day Delilah	Van Stephenson	27	9
6/6/81	7/25/81	Modern Girl	Sheena Easton	18	15
6/7/86	7/12/86	Modern Woman	Billy Joel	19	12
1/12/80	2/9/80	Money	Flying Lizards	18	11
7/20/85	8/31/85	Money For Nothing	Dire Straits	1	20
8/16/86	9/6/86	Money$ Too Tight (To Mention)	Simply Red	26	8
7/9/88	9/3/88	Monkey	George Michael	1	13
9/5/87	11/21/87	Mony Mony "Live"	Billy Idol	1	22
3/24/90	4/7/90	Moonlight On Water	Laura Branigan	26	4
6/13/87	7/25/87	Moonlighting	Al Jarreau	17	10
7/19/80	9/6/80	More Love	Kim Carnes	14	15
11/8/80	12/27/80	More Than I Can Say	Leo Sayer	8	20
3/11/89	4/1/89	More Than You Know	Martika	18	5
3/28/81	5/2/81	Morning Train (Nine To Five)	Sheena Easton	1	22
5/10/86	5/31/86	Mothers Talk	Tears For Fears	24	6
5/24/86	6/28/86	Mountains	Prince & the Revolution	15	10
4/5/86	5/3/86	Move Away	Culture Club	22	11
7/25/87	8/8/87	Mr. Perfect For Me	Natalie Archangel	39	3
2/5/83	3/12/83	Mr. Roboto	Styx	1	26
1/26/85	3/2/85	Mr. Telephone Man	New Edition	6	10

Debut	Peak	Title	Artist	Pos	Wks
12/11/82	1/8/83	Muscles	Diana Ross	26	9
2/21/87	3/14/87	My Baby	Pretenders	'24	4
4/17/82	5/22/82	My Girl	Donnie Iris	33	12
3/4/89	4/1/89	My Heart Can't Tell You No	Rod Stewart	12	6
12/14/85	1/18/86	My Hometown	Bruce Springsteen	6	14
2/26/83	3/19/83	My Kind Of Lady	Supertramp	34	9
11/21/81	12/19/81	My Kinda Lover	Billy Squier	19	13
5/28/83	6/25/83	My Love	Lionel Richie	20	10
10/15/88	12/3/88	My Prerogative	Bobby Brown	7	14
7/28/79	8/18/79	My Sharona	Knack	1	27
8/3/85	8/31/85	Mystery Lady	Billy Ocean	26	8
6/7/86	7/12/86	Nasty	Janet Jackson	3	15
4/23/88	6/4/88	Naughty Girls (Need Love Too)	Samantha Fox	2	15
2/16/85	3/23/85	Naughty Naughty	John Parr	30	8
10/24/87	12/19/87	Need You Tonight	INXS	7	17
2/1/86	3/1/86	Needles And Pins	Tom Petty & the Heartbreakers with Stevie Nicks	22	8
1/19/85	2/23/85	Neutron Dance	Pointer Sisters	7	15
9/28/85	12/7/85	Never	Heart	10	17
4/19/86	5/17/86	Never As Good As The First Time	Sade	33	7
10/11/80	11/22/80	Never Be The Same	Christopher Cross	20	19
6/1/85	7/13/85	Never Ending Story	Limahl	17	10
4/9/83	5/7/83	Never Give Up	Sammy Hagar	35	7
2/6/88	3/26/88	Never Gonna Give You Up	Rick Astley	1	17
6/11/83	8/20/83	Never Gonna Let You Go	Sergio Mendes	2	20
11/1/80	11/29/80	Never Knew Love Like This Before	Stephanie Mills	11	16
6/8/85	8/3/85	Never Surrender	Corey Hart	3	18
9/17/88	10/15/88	Never Tear Us Apart	INXS	13	5
4/27/85	5/25/85	New Attitude	Patti LaBelle	13	12
2/4/84	3/17/84	New Moon On Monday	Duran Duran	11	17
6/4/88	7/16/88	New Sensation	INXS	5	8
3/31/84	4/28/84	New Song	Howard Jones	18	11
9/25/82	10/16/82	New World Man	Rush	15	14
9/20/86	12/6/86	Next Time I Fall, The	Peter Cetera with Amy Grant	6	17
8/15/81	10/10/81	Nicole	Point Blank	9	18

Debut	Peak	Title	Artist	Pos	Wks
10/26/85	12/7/85	Night Is Still Young, The	Billy Joel	41	7
2/8/86	3/29/86	Night Moves	Marilyn Martin	42	8
10/3/81	11/14/81	Night Owls, The	Little River Band	5	20
8/20/88	9/24/88	Nightmare On My Street, A	D.J. Jazzy Jeff & the Fresh Prince	2	8
5/13/89	6/3/89	Nightrain	Guns N' Roses	18	5
3/30/85	4/27/85	Nightshift	Commodores	6	14
1/18/86	3/29/86	Nikita	Elton John	15	17
1/17/81	3/7/81	9 To 5	Dolly Parton	1	25
6/1/85	6/29/85	19	Paul Hardcastle	8	13
7/9/83	9/10/83	1999	Prince	6	20
1/28/84	2/25/84	99 Luftballons	Nena	1	6
1/28/84	2/25/84	99 Red Balloons	Nena	1	17
6/4/88	7/2/88	Nite And Day	Al B. Sure!	7	8
9/12/81	10/17/81	(There's) No Gettin' Over Me	Ronnie Milsap	19	12
8/10/85	9/14/85	No Lookin' Back	Michael McDonald	36	7
10/13/84	11/24/84	No More Lonely Nights	Paul McCartney	10	16
11/3/79	12/1/79	No More Tears (Enough Is Enough)	Barbra Streisand & Donna Summer	2	18
5/19/84	6/9/84	No More Words	Berlin	21	11
3/3/90	3/31/90	No Myth	Michael Penn	10	8
10/4/80	10/25/80	No Night So Long	Dionne Warwick	27	9
3/29/86	6/7/86	No One Is To Blame	Howard Jones	10	19
5/15/82	7/10/82	No One Like You	Scorpions	26	24
10/24/81	11/21/81	No Reply At All	Genesis	11	17
11/14/87	11/28/87	No Such Thing	Tommy Shaw	34	3
9/26/87	10/10/87	No Surrender	Outfield	34	4
9/5/81	10/24/81	No Time To Lose	Tarney/Spencer Band	24	16
6/23/84	7/21/84	No Way Out	Jefferson Starship	25	10
11/13/82	11/27/82	Nobody	Sylvia	19	14
1/28/84	2/18/84	Nobody Told Me	John Lennon	11	13
1/24/87	2/21/87	Nobody's Fool	Cinderella	13	6
7/30/88	8/20/88	Nobody's Fool	Kenny Loggins	21	5
6/4/83	6/18/83	Not Now John	Pink Floyd	31	8
4/26/86	5/31/86	Nothin' At All	Heart	19	12
4/16/88	6/4/88	Nothin' But A Good Time	Poison	6	11
3/24/90	4/28/90	Nothing Compares 2 U	Sinead O'Connor	1	7
7/26/86	9/13/86	Nothing In Common	Thompson Twins	29	9
2/28/87	5/23/87	Nothing's Gonna Change My Love For You	Glenn Medeiros	4	20

Debut	Peak	Title	Artist	Pos	Wks
2/7/87	4/11/87	Nothing's Gonna Stop Us Now	Starship	1	16
11/15/86	1/17/87	Notorious	Duran Duran	2	13
9/5/87	9/12/87	Notorious	Loverboy	36	3
7/14/84	7/28/84	Obscene Phone Caller	Rockwell	25	6
3/23/85	4/27/85	Obsession	Animotion	7	16
4/5/80	5/3/80	Off The Wall	Michael Jackson	21	13
7/29/89	8/26/89	Oh Daddy	Adrian Belew	10	8
12/19/81	1/9/82	Oh No	Commodores	21	10
9/7/85	10/12/85	Oh Sheila	Ready For The World	1	16
4/14/84	5/12/84	Oh Sherrie	Steve Perry	7	17
7/4/87	9/26/87	Oh Yeah	Yello	4	19
2/9/85	3/9/85	Old Man Down The Road, The	John Fogerty	17	11
11/21/81	12/19/81	Old Songs, The	Barry Manilow	18	10
10/8/83	11/12/83	Old Time Rock & Roll	Bob Seger & the Silver Bullet Band	5	17
4/26/86	5/31/86	On My Own	Patti LaBelle & Michael McDonald	1	18
7/29/89	9/2/89	On Our Own	Bobby Brown	5	9
9/22/84	11/10/84	On The Dark Side	John Cafferty & the Beaver Brown Band	15	16
1/15/83	2/5/83	On The Loose	Saga	25	14
2/2/80	3/15/80	On The Radio	Donna Summer	5	18
1/8/83	1/29/83	On The Wings Of Love	Jeffrey Osborne	26	9
6/17/89	7/22/89	Once Bitten Twice Shy	Great White	1	14
5/13/89	5/27/89	One	Metallica	13	5
7/5/80	8/9/80	One Fine Day	Carole King	18	11
8/20/88	9/24/88	One Good Woman	Peter Cetera	9	7
9/5/87	10/3/87	One Heartbeat	Smokey Robinson	12	8
10/31/87	12/5/87	One I Love, The	R.E.M.	7	9
8/9/80	8/30/80	One In A Million You	Larry Graham	24	14
3/30/85	4/27/85	One Lonely Night	REO Speedwagon	38	11
9/24/88	11/12/88	One Moment In Time	Whitney Houston	6	11
2/9/85	3/30/85	One More Night	Phil Collins	3	18
4/30/88	6/11/88	One More Try	George Michael	1	16
3/16/85	4/27/85	One Night In Bangkok	Murray Head	5	17
9/14/85	11/9/85	One Night Love Affair	Bryan Adams	23	12
10/12/85	11/23/85	One Of The Living	Tina Turner	22	11
3/5/83	3/26/83	One On One	Daryl Hall & John Oates	11	15

Debut	Peak	Title	Artist	Pos	Wks
12/20/80	1/24/81	One Step Closer	Doobie Brothers	35	8
7/19/86	8/23/86	One Step Closer To You	Gavin Christopher	31	9
6/20/81	8/1/81	One That You Love, The	Air Supply	6	21
6/4/83	6/18/83	One Thing, The	INXS	29	8
9/17/83	10/29/83	One Thing Leads To Another	Fixx	11	20
7/2/88	8/6/88	1-2-3	Gloria Estefan & Miami Sound Machine	3	11
10/9/82	11/6/82	One You Love, The	Glenn Frey	12	15
5/30/87	9/5/87	Only In My Dreams	Debbie Gibson	3	27
5/8/82	8/14/82	Only The Lonely	Motels	7	23
1/26/85	2/23/85	Only The Young	Journey	23	10
8/7/82	9/18/82	Only Time Will Tell	Asia	9	14
4/14/90	5/5/90	Ooh La La (I Can't Get Over You)	Perfect Gentlemen	20	4
1/16/82	3/13/82	Open Arms	Journey	4	23
12/13/86	2/14/87	Open Your Heart	Madonna	3	14
6/14/86	8/2/86	Opportunities (Let's Make Lots Of Money)	Pet Shop Boys	25	11
1/13/90	2/17/90	Opposites Attract	Paula Abdul with the Wild Pair	1	17
1/8/83	2/5/83	Other Guy, The	Little River Band	14	11
8/23/86	9/27/86	Other Side Of Life, The	Moody Blues	46	6
5/15/82	6/19/82	Other Woman, The	Ray Parker, Jr.	3	18
6/4/83	7/16/83	Our House	Madness	10	18
12/26/81	2/13/82	Our Lips Are Sealed	Go-Go's	2	25
5/10/86	6/28/86	Out Of Mind Out Of Sight	Models	25	10
2/13/88	4/9/88	Out Of The Blue	Debbie Gibson	2	16
10/13/84	11/24/84	Out Of Touch	Daryl Hall & John Oates	8	18
7/24/82	9/4/82	Out Of Work	Gary U.S. Bonds	11	13
3/1/86	4/19/86	Overjoyed	Stevie Wonder	20	11
4/23/83	5/21/83	Overkill	Men At Work	6	17
11/26/83	1/7/84	Owner Of A Lonely Heart	Yes	4	21
2/13/82	4/10/82	Pac-Man Fever	Buckner & Garcia	3	19
7/28/84	8/18/84	Panama	Van Halen	23	9
6/28/86	7/26/86	Papa Don't Preach	Madonna	1	18
10/3/87	10/17/87	Paper In Fire	John Cougar Mellencamp	25	4
6/5/82	7/10/82	Paperlate	Genesis	11	15
1/14/89	3/11/89	Paradise City	Guns N' Roses	4	16
8/23/86	10/4/86	Paranoimia	Art Of Noise with Max Headroom	29	9

Debut	Peak	Title	Artist	Pos	Wks
7/9/88	8/13/88	Parents Just Don't Understand	D.J. Jazzy Jeff & the Fresh Prince	3	9
9/7/85	11/2/85	Part-Time Lover	Stevie Wonder	4	19
11/16/85	12/21/85	Party All The Time	Eddie Murphy	3	18
3/7/81	4/25/81	Party's Over (Hopelessly In Love), The	Journey	24	13
2/5/83	2/26/83	Pass The Dutchie	Musical Youth	8	13
12/20/80	1/24/81	Passion	Rod Stewart	15	15
3/18/89	5/27/89	Patience	Guns N' Roses	1	21
12/9/89	2/3/90	Peace In Our Time	Eddie Money	9	14
10/6/84	11/10/84	Penny Lover	Lionel Richie	18	16
6/29/85	8/3/85	People Are People	Depeche Mode	10	13
10/19/85	12/21/85	Perfect Way	Scritti Politti	18	17
7/30/88	8/27/88	Perfect World	Huey Lewis & the News	15	5
7/10/82	7/31/82	Personally	Karla Bonoff	19	13
3/26/83	5/14/83	Photograph	Def Leppard	7	21
10/24/81	12/5/81	Physical	Olivia Newton-John	1	30
5/10/80	5/31/80	Pilot Of The Airwaves	Charlie Dore	20	12
8/12/89	8/26/89	Pinball Wizard	Elton John	24	3
3/5/88	4/30/88	Pink Cadillac	Natalie Cole	1	18
1/7/84	2/18/84	Pink Houses	John Cougar Mellencamp	17	13
2/13/88	4/9/88	Play That Funky Music	Roxanne	17	9
5/22/82	7/3/82	Play The Game Tonight	Kansas	17	17
11/17/79	1/12/80	Please Don't Go	KC & the Sunshine Band	3	21
9/3/88	10/8/88	Please Don't Go Girl	New Kids On The Block	11	7
7/11/87	8/8/87	Pleasure Principle, The	Janet Jackson	14	9
5/23/87	7/18/87	Point Of No Return	Expose	7	15
4/21/90	5/5/90	Poison	Bell Biv DeVoe	16	3
10/28/89	11/25/89	Poison	Alice Cooper	7	11
3/19/83	4/16/83	Poison Arrow	ABC	22	11
10/31/81	12/19/81	Poor Man's Son	Survivor	16	17
12/26/87	2/13/88	Pop Goes The World	Men Without Hats	9	9
7/27/85	8/31/85	Pop Life	Prince & the Revolution	11	12
9/29/79	12/22/79	Pop Muzik	M	3	23
5/7/88	7/16/88	Pour Some Sugar On Me	Def Leppard	1	19
6/29/85	8/3/85	Power Of Love, The	Huey Lewis & the News	2	19
8/16/86	9/20/86	Press	Paul McCartney	14	9
10/16/82	11/13/82	Pressure	Billy Joel	12	15
2/13/82	3/20/82	(Oh) Pretty Woman	Van Halen	8	21

Debut	Peak	Title	Artist	Pos	Wks
3/17/90	4/7/90	Price Of Love	Bad English	15	5
12/15/84	1/12/85	Pride (In The Name Of Love)	U2	21	9
7/22/89	7/29/89	Pride & Passion	John Cafferty & the Beaver Brown Band	27	2
5/16/87	6/6/87	Primitive Love Rites	Mondo Rock	37	4
3/23/85	4/20/85	Private Dancer	Tina Turner	23	8
9/5/81	11/7/81	Private Eyes	Daryl Hall & John Oates	1	29
8/9/86	9/20/86	Private Number	Jets	36	8
10/22/88	11/12/88	Promise, The	When In Rome	25	6
8/20/83	10/22/83	Promises, Promises	Naked Eyes	7	18
4/23/88	5/21/88	Prove Your Love	Taylor Dayne	15	8
11/4/89	12/9/89	Pump Up The Jam	Technotronic featuring Felly	1	27
1/2/88	2/13/88	Pump Up The Volume	M/A/R/R/S	1	17
1/21/89	2/18/89	Purple Haze	Robert Palmer	15	6
10/6/84	11/3/84	Purple Rain	Prince & the Revolution	2	18
1/30/88	3/5/88	Push It	Salt-N-Pepa	2	12
12/31/88	1/21/89	Put A Little Love In Your Heart	Annie Lennox & Al Green	21	4
8/13/83	9/17/83	Puttin' On The Ritz	Taco	2	18
11/26/83	12/24/83	P.Y.T. (Pretty Young Thing)	Michael Jackson	16	17
7/11/81	10/10/81	Queen Of Hearts	Juice Newton	4	27
10/15/83	11/5/83	Queen Of The Broken Hearts	Loverboy	29	8
3/24/84	4/14/84	Radio Ga-Ga	Queen	19	10
4/13/85	5/4/85	Radioactive	Firm	24	8
6/25/88	7/30/88	Rag Doll	Aerosmith	7	10
10/25/86	11/15/86	Rain, The	Oran "Juice" Jones	5	12
5/17/86	6/7/86	Rain On The Scarecrow	John Cougar Mellencamp	21	7
11/10/79	12/22/79	Rapper's Delight	Sugarhill Gang	17	18
2/21/81	4/25/81	Rapture	Blondie	2	17
5/18/85	7/20/85	Raspberry Beret	Prince & the Revolution	4	17
2/9/80	3/8/80	Ravel's Bolero	Henry Mancini	15	12
12/24/83	1/14/84	Read 'Em And Weep	Barry Manilow	30	10
9/6/80	10/25/80	Real Love	Doobie Brothers	8	20
4/1/89	5/20/89	Real Love	Jody Watley	8	10
8/29/81	9/26/81	Really Wanna Know You	Gary Wright	20	9
9/3/88	10/15/88	Red Red Wine	UB40	1	14

Debut	Peak	Title	Artist	Pos	Wks
5/12/84	6/16/84	Reflex, The	Duran Duran	1	18
3/15/80	4/12/80	Refugee	Tom Petty & the Heartbreakers	13	17
1/26/85	3/23/85	Relax	Frankie Goes To Hollywood	7	17
12/27/86	3/14/87	Respect Yourself	Bruce Willis	8	13
6/13/87	7/25/87	Rhythm Is Gonna Get You	Gloria Estefan & Miami Sound Machine	6	10
12/2/89	1/13/90	Rhythm Nation	Janet Jackson	9	13
4/23/88	6/11/88	Rhythm Of Love	Scorpions	15	9
3/30/85	4/27/85	Rhythm Of The Night	DeBarge	3	15
3/29/80	5/17/80	Ride Like The Wind	Christopher Cross	2	25
5/17/86	6/14/86	Right And Wrong	Joe Jackson	28	8
5/10/86	5/31/86	Right Between The Eyes	Wax	27	6
9/15/84	9/22/84	Right By Your Side	Eurythmics	34	5
7/8/89	8/26/89	Right Here Waiting	Richard Marx	1	16
3/21/87	5/2/87	Right On Track	Breakfast Club	10	9
9/8/79	10/27/79	Rise	Herb Alpert	1	23
7/18/87	8/8/87	River Of Love	Trance Dance	31	4
12/20/86	1/24/87	Roadrunner (Radio On)	Joan Jett & the Blackhearts	34	6
1/13/90	3/10/90	Roam	B-52's	4	17
12/19/87	2/13/88	Rock And Roll All Nite	Poison	11	10
6/27/81	8/1/81	Rock And Roll Dreams Come Through	Jim Steinman	17	17
4/6/85	5/11/85	Rock And Roll Girls	John Fogerty	15	13
2/1/86	3/29/86	R.O.C.K. In The U.S.A.	John Cougar Mellencamp	5	16
5/24/80	6/14/80	Rock Lobster	B-52's	20	12
2/15/86	3/29/86	Rock Me Amadeus	Falco	1	17
8/6/83	9/10/83	Rock 'N' Roll Is King	Electric Light Orchestra	8	13
6/25/83	8/6/83	Rock Of Ages	Def Leppard	6	19
2/13/88	3/12/88	Rock Of Life	Rick Springfield	18	6
4/1/89	6/24/89	Rock On	Michael Damian	1	20
6/27/87	8/15/87	Rock Steady	Whispers	7	16
12/11/82	1/22/83	Rock The Casbah	Clash	6	18
5/9/87	6/27/87	Rock The Night	Europe	23	9
11/6/82	12/25/82	Rock This Town	Stray Cats	4	20
10/21/89	11/11/89	Rock Wit'cha	Bobby Brown	11	7
12/29/79	2/9/80	Rock With You	Michael Jackson	1	24
3/31/84	5/5/84	Rock You Like A Hurricane	Scorpions	12	16
3/18/89	4/29/89	Rocket	Def Leppard	8	8
2/27/88	4/16/88	Rocket 2 U	Jets	3	11

Debut	Peak	Title	Artist	Pos	Wks
2/2/85	2/16/85	Rockin' At Midnight	Honeydrippers	27	7
6/4/83	7/2/83	Roll Me Away	Bob Seger & the Silver Bullet Band	28	10
6/11/88	8/6/88	Roll With It	Steve Winwood	1	14
2/9/80	3/15/80	Romeo's Tune	Steve Forbert	12	13
2/4/89	3/18/89	Roni	Bobby Brown	10	10
5/8/82	7/3/82	Rosanna	Toto	3	22
5/17/80	6/28/80	Rose, The	Bette Midler	2	23
3/29/86	5/3/86	Rough Boy	ZZ Top	33	8
7/28/84	8/25/84	Round And Round	Ratt	8	13
6/3/89	7/15/89	Route 66	Depeche Mode	7	9
6/28/86	8/16/86	Rumbleseat	John Cougar Mellencamp	25	11
8/2/86	8/30/86	Rumors	Timex Social Club	4	13
5/29/82	6/26/82	Run For The Roses	Dan Fogelberg	31	9
12/8/84	1/26/85	Run To You	Bryan Adams	9	14
2/25/84	4/14/84	Runner	Manfred Mann's Earth Band	16	14
8/12/89	9/9/89	Runnin' Down A Dream	Tom Petty	12	7
1/7/84	2/4/84	Running With The Night	Lionel Richie	14	16
5/14/88	6/25/88	Rush Hour	Jane Wiedlin	15	7
1/25/86	3/8/86	Russians	Sting	16	12
7/8/89	8/5/89	Sacred Emotion	Donny Osmond	20	6
2/17/90	3/17/90	Sacrifice	Elton John	6	12
8/18/79	9/29/79	Sad Eyes	Robert John	2	24
6/23/84	7/28/84	Sad Songs (Say So Much)	Elton John	9	14
8/27/83	9/24/83	Safety Dance, The	Men Without Hats	1	20
9/15/79	11/3/79	Sail On	Commodores	5	20
8/2/80	9/6/80	Sailing	Christopher Cross	2	20
7/30/83	9/10/83	Salt In My Tears, The	Martin Briley	20	13
5/2/87	6/6/87	Same Ole Love (365 Days A Year)	Anita Baker	21	7
1/25/86	3/8/86	Sanctify Yourself	Simple Minds	19	12
1/19/80	2/9/80	Sara	Fleetwood Mac	10	13
1/11/86	3/15/86	Sara	Starship	5	16
5/6/89	6/24/89	Satisfied	Richard Marx	8	11
10/31/81	12/5/81	Sausalito Summernight	Diesel	18	11
2/2/85	2/23/85	Save A Prayer	Duran Duran	22	11
7/23/83	8/13/83	Saved By Zero	Fixx	21	15
9/21/85	11/9/85	Saving All My Love For You	Whitney Houston	2	15

Debut	Peak	Title	Artist	Pos	Wks
2/20/82	4/24/82	Say Goodbye	Triumph	43	13
9/12/81	10/24/81	Say Goodbye To Hollywood	Billy Joel	20	15
11/19/83	1/14/84	Say It Isn't So	Daryl Hall & John Oates	9	16
10/15/83	12/10/83	Say Say Say	Paul McCartney & Michael Jackson	2	24
7/18/87	8/15/87	Say You Really Want Me	Kim Wilde	30	6
11/2/85	12/28/85	Say You, Say Me	Lionel Richie	1	21
1/30/88	2/20/88	Say You Will	Foreigner	14	5
5/4/85	5/25/85	Say You're Wrong	Julian Lennon	25	9
3/28/87	5/2/87	Se La	Lionel Richie	20	6
11/10/84	12/22/84	Sea Of Love	Honeydrippers	4	16
5/18/85	6/29/85	Search Is Over, The	Survivor	22	14
9/5/81	10/3/81	Searchin'	Santana	34	8
2/20/88	3/5/88	Seasons Change	Expose	12	9
5/13/89	5/20/89	Second Chance	.38 Special	20	3
3/1/80	3/29/80	Second Time Around, The	Shalamar	15	13
2/15/86	4/5/86	Secret Lovers	Atlantic Starr	3	15
8/5/89	8/26/89	Secret Rendezvous	Karyn White	15	6
6/7/86	7/26/86	Secret Separation	Fixx	16	12
6/2/84	7/14/84	Self Control	Laura Branigan	4	16
10/22/83	11/19/83	Send Her My Love	Journey	36	9
5/27/89	7/8/89	Send Me An Angel	Real Life	8	8
12/1/79	1/19/80	Send One Your Love	Stevie Wonder	20	13
4/28/90	5/5/90	Sending All My Love	Linear	22	2
6/8/85	8/10/85	Sentimental Street	Night Ranger	14	15
10/5/85	11/30/85	Separate Lives	Phil Collins & Marilyn Martin	1	23
1/29/83	3/12/83	Separate Ways (Worlds Apart)	Journey	6	19
2/9/80	3/15/80	September Morn'	Neil Diamond	17	14
4/11/87	5/9/87	Serious	Donna Allen	20	6
1/31/87	3/28/87	Set Me Free (Rosa Lee)	Los Lobos	22	9
9/1/84	9/15/84	17	Rick James	29	6
12/11/82	1/15/83	Sexual Healing	Marvin Gaye	11	18
9/17/83	10/1/83	(She's) Sexy + 17	Stray Cats	13	12
4/19/80	6/14/80	Sexy Eyes	Dr. Hook	10	20
7/28/84	9/1/84	Sexy Girl	Glenn Frey	13	10
10/23/82	11/27/82	Shadows Of The Night	Pat Benatar	7	20
12/19/81	2/13/82	Shake It Up	Cars	6	20
11/29/86	1/24/87	Shake You Down	Gregory Abbott	4	13

Debut	Peak	Title	Artist	Pos	Wks
10/31/87	12/26/87	Shake Your Love	Debbie Gibson	5	15
10/15/88	12/10/88	Shake Your Thang	Salt-N-Pepa	10	10
5/23/87	8/8/87	Shakedown	Bob Seger	2	17
12/18/82	2/26/83	Shame On The Moon	Bob Seger & the Silver Bullet Band	2	24
10/17/81	11/7/81	Share Your Love With Me	Kenny Rogers	34	8
4/2/88	6/4/88	Shattered Dreams	Johnny Hates Jazz	1	14
5/7/83	5/28/83	She Blinded Me With Science	Thomas Dolby	4	16
8/25/84	9/29/84	She Bop	Cyndi Lauper	2	17
1/28/89	3/18/89	She Drives Me Crazy	Fine Young Cannibals	5	14
12/10/88	2/4/89	She Wants To Dance With Me	Rick Astley	2	14
8/6/83	9/10/83	She Works Hard For The Money	Donna Summer	2	17
12/27/86	1/10/87	Shelter	Lone Justice	53	3
4/30/83	6/11/83	She's A Beauty	Tubes	9	17
2/20/88	3/26/88	She's Like The Wind	Patrick Swayze (featuring Wendy Fraser)	4	11
2/27/88	4/2/88	She's Only 20	Tami Show	22	6
11/29/80	12/13/80	She's So Cold	Rolling Stones	35	7
9/29/84	10/13/84	Shine Shine	Barry Gibb	28	5
7/26/80	8/30/80	Shining Star	Manhattans	15	12
3/14/87	4/4/87	Ship Of Fools (Save Me From Tomorrow)	World Party	24	5
10/13/79	12/8/79	Ships	Barry Manilow	13	17
11/20/82	12/25/82	Shock The Monkey	Peter Gabriel	14	15
3/6/82	4/17/82	Should I Do It	Pointer Sisters	30	13
9/26/87	12/5/87	Should've Known Better	Richard Marx	4	13
6/29/85	7/27/85	Shout	Tears For Fears	1	16
4/28/84	5/12/84	Show Me	Pretenders	29	7
5/25/85	6/8/85	Show Some Respect	Tina Turner	35	6
8/12/89	9/16/89	Shower Me With Your Love	Surface	6	10
11/23/85	1/18/86	Sidewalk Talk	Jellybean	19	16
4/11/87	5/2/87	Sign 'O' The Times	Prince	17	5
1/21/84	2/4/84	Sign Of Fire, The	Fixx	39	5
7/23/88	8/20/88	Sign Your Name	Terence Trent D'Arby	10	8
11/16/85	3/1/86	Silent Running (On Dangerous Ground)	Mike + the Mechanics	14	22
7/9/88	9/17/88	Simply Irresistible	Robert Palmer	1	13
4/17/82	5/15/82	Since You're Gone	Cars	21	10
7/11/87	8/22/87	Since You've Been Gone	Outfield	15	9

Debut	Peak	Title	Artist	Pos	Wks
4/1/89	4/29/89	Sincerely Yours	Sweet Sensation	10	6
4/23/83	5/28/83	Sing Me Away	Night Ranger	40	9
5/12/84	6/23/84	Sister Christian	Night Ranger	2	15
10/1/83	10/22/83	Sitting At The Wheel	Moody Blues	25	8
2/7/87	3/7/87	Six	Madhouse	23	5
4/17/82	6/5/82	'65 Love Affair	Paul Davis	2	19
6/7/86	7/19/86	Sledgehammer	Peter Gabriel	2	16
10/19/85	11/23/85	Sleeping Bag	ZZ Top	12	16
7/2/83	7/23/83	Slipping Away	Dave Edmunds	25	12
7/25/81	8/29/81	Slow Hand	Pointer Sisters	7	18
11/2/85	12/21/85	Small Town	John Cougar Mellencamp	11	17
8/17/85	9/14/85	Smokin' In The Boys Room	Motley Crue	10	11
3/14/87	4/18/87	Smoking Gun	Robert Cray Band	9	6
12/17/88	1/14/89	Smooth Criminal	Michael Jackson	9	7
4/20/85	6/8/85	Smooth Operator	Sade	7	13
5/18/85	6/29/85	Smuggler's Blues	Glenn Frey	10	13
6/17/89	7/29/89	So Alive	Love And Rockets	3	15
10/24/87	12/5/87	So Emotional	Whitney Houston	11	13
3/8/86	4/5/86	So Far Away	Dire Straits	24	9
7/19/86	9/27/86	So Far So Good	Sheena Easton	31	13
10/5/85	11/23/85	So In Love	Orchestral Manoeuvres In The Dark	21	11
11/12/83	1/14/84	So Many Men - So Little Time	Miquel Brown	18	21
5/14/83	6/4/83	So Wrong	Patrick Simmons	24	9
3/25/89	6/3/89	Soldier Of Love	Donny Osmond	3	13
2/9/85	3/23/85	Solid	Ashford & Simpson	12	12
4/30/83	6/4/83	Solitaire	Laura Branigan	15	13
11/3/84	11/24/84	Some Guys Have All The Luck	Rod Stewart	31	8
3/16/85	5/4/85	Some Like It Hot	Power Station	10	17
3/23/85	4/27/85	Some Things Are Better Left Unsaid	Daryl Hall & John Oates	28	10
3/9/85	4/6/85	Somebody	Bryan Adams	18	11
8/28/82	10/2/82	Somebody's Baby	Jackson Browne	6	16
10/18/86	11/22/86	Somebody's Out There	Triumph	36	9
2/18/84	3/24/84	Somebody's Watching Me	Rockwell	1	16
11/22/86	1/24/87	Someday	Glass Tiger	10	12
3/29/86	6/14/86	Something About You	Level 42	8	19
7/4/87	7/25/87	Something So Strong	Crowded House	21	5
10/11/80	11/15/80	Sometimes A Fantasy	Billy Joel	25	11

Debut	Peak	Title	Artist	Pos	Wks
11/25/89	3/10/90	Sometimes She Cries	Warrant	7	16
8/1/87	8/15/87	Sometimes The Good Guys Finish First	Pat Benatar	40	3
1/24/87	3/21/87	Somewhere Out There	Linda Ronstadt & James Ingram	3	13
5/2/87	7/4/87	Songbird	Kenny G	2	15
10/5/85	11/9/85	Soul Kiss	Olivia Newton-John	15	12
10/9/82	12/4/82	Southern Cross	Crosby, Stills & Nash	22	18
12/25/82	1/29/83	Space Age Love Song	Flock Of Seagulls	18	12
2/23/80	4/5/80	Special Lady	Ray, Goodman & Brown	8	19
11/30/85	2/1/86	Spies Like Us	Paul McCartney	7	16
3/29/80	4/26/80	Spirit Of Radio, The	Rush	16	12
12/12/87	1/30/88	Spotlight	Madonna	15	9
7/6/85	8/24/85	St. Elmo's Fire (Man In Motion)	John Parr	1	20
1/18/86	2/15/86	Stages	ZZ Top	25	12
1/28/89	3/4/89	Stand	R.E.M.	3	10
6/18/83	8/20/83	Stand Back	Stevie Nicks	12	19
11/1/86	12/27/86	Stand By Me	Ben E. King	2	15
5/16/81	6/13/81	Stars On 45	Stars On 45	2	18
8/22/81	10/3/81	Start Me Up	Rolling Stones	2	30
11/15/80	12/27/80	(Just Like) Starting Over	John Lennon	1	26
6/30/84	8/4/84	State Of Shock	Jacksons	6	13
3/29/80	5/10/80	Stay In Time	Off Broadway	9	19
6/2/84	6/30/84	Stay The Night	Chicago	16	14
12/13/86	1/10/87	Stay The Night	Benjamin Orr	37	5
6/7/80	7/19/80	Steal Away	Robbie Dupree	4	20
9/19/81	10/31/81	Step By Step	Eddie Rabbitt	8	15
10/9/82	11/13/82	Steppin' Out	Joe Jackson	2	18
4/5/86	5/17/86	Stick Around	Julian Lennon	23	10
11/3/79	12/15/79	Still	Commodores	5	19
4/24/82	5/22/82	Still In Saigon	Charlie Daniels Band	16	11
5/22/82	7/3/82	Still They Ride	Journey	22	13
4/19/80	6/7/80	Stomp	Brothers Johnson	20	13
4/4/87	5/2/87	Stone Love	Kool & the Gang	15	6
8/1/81	9/26/81	Stop Draggin' My Heart Around	Stevie Nicks with Tom Petty & the Heartbreakers	7	21
8/20/83	8/20/83	Stop In The Name Of Love	Hollies	39	5
11/29/80	2/14/81	Stop This Game	Cheap Trick	27	15
4/23/83	5/14/83	Straight From The Heart	Bryan Adams	13	16
1/14/89	2/25/89	Straight Up	Paula Abdul	1	17

Debut	Peak	Title	Artist	Pos	Wks
3/19/88	4/30/88	Strange But True	X2	22	8
8/8/81	9/5/81	Stranger	Jefferson Starship	37	7
12/8/84	1/12/85	Stranger In Town	Toto	37	7
1/15/83	2/19/83	Stray Cat Strut	Stray Cats	4	18
5/23/81	7/25/81	Stroke, The	Billy Squier	1	29
10/20/84	12/1/84	Strut	Sheena Easton	3	17
7/21/84	8/18/84	Stuck On You	Lionel Richie	5	14
8/2/86	9/20/86	Stuck With You	Huey Lewis & the News	3	17
5/11/85	6/15/85	Suddenly	Billy Ocean	5	13
10/22/83	11/19/83	Suddenly Last Summer	Motels	15	13
2/2/85	3/2/85	Sugar Walls	Sheena Easton	11	11
5/16/81	6/20/81	Sukiyaki	Taste of Honey	7	14
2/6/82	3/20/82	Summer Nights	Survivor	30	12
6/29/85	8/17/85	Summer Of '69	Bryan Adams	9	16
12/28/85	2/15/86	Sun Always Shines On T.V., The	a-ha	24	12
8/4/84	9/8/84	Sunglasses At Night	Corey Hart	5	13
9/7/85	10/5/85	Sunset Grill	Don Henley	26	10
12/21/85	1/11/86	Superbowl Shuffle	Chicago Bears Shufflin' Crew	1	14
11/29/86	12/27/86	Superman	R.E.M.	24	7
4/9/88	5/28/88	Supersonic	J.J. Fad	12	9
2/25/89	4/1/89	Superwoman	Karyn White	8	7
3/4/89	3/18/89	Surrender To Me	Ann Wilson & Robin Zander	22	3
5/11/85	7/20/85	Sussudio	Phil Collins	2	17
6/21/86	7/19/86	Suzanne	Journey	36	8
7/30/88	9/10/88	Sweet Child O' Mine	Guns N' Roses	1	13
2/6/82	4/17/82	Sweet Dreams	Air Supply	17	17
7/23/83	9/3/83	Sweet Dreams (Are Made Of This)	Eurythmics	1	19
6/14/86	8/30/86	Sweet Freedom	Michael McDonald	·11	17
9/27/86	11/1/86	Sweet Love	Anita Baker	16	13
10/2/82	10/23/82	Sweet Time	REO Speedwagon	20	9
1/11/86	2/22/86	Sweetest Taboo, The	Sade	9	14
1/16/82	2/20/82	Sweetest Thing (I've Ever Known), The	Juice Newton	15	11
5/23/81	7/25/81	Sweetheart	Franke & the Knockouts	16	16
10/27/84	11/10/84	Swept Away	Diana Ross	23	8
9/23/89	11/4/89	Swing The Mood	Jive Bunny & the Mastermixers	1	9
4/16/83	5/14/83	Swingin'	John Anderson	12	14
10/11/80	1/17/81	Switchin' To Glide	Kings	9	24

Debut	Peak	Title	Artist	Pos	Wks
11/5/83	12/3/83	Synchronicity II	Police	18	15
2/6/82	5/1/82	Tainted Love	Soft Cell	9	34
8/23/80	9/6/80	Take A Little Rhythm	Ali Thomson	36	7
7/24/82	9/4/82	Take It Away	Paul McCartney	13	15
2/20/82	3/27/82	Take It Easy On Me	Little River Band	19	16
3/21/81	5/16/81	Take It On The Run	REO Speedwagon	5	21
3/22/86	4/26/86	Take Me Home	Phil Collins	10	15
9/20/86	11/29/86	Take Me Home Tonight	Eddie Money	6	17
7/23/83	8/20/83	Take Me To Heart	Quarterflash	22	14
3/9/85	3/23/85	Take Me With U	Prince & the Revolution	31	6
7/19/86	9/27/86	Take My Breath Away	Berlin	8	17
12/26/81	1/23/82	Take My Heart (You Can Have It If You Want It)	Kool & the Gang	31	8
2/13/82	3/13/82	Take Off	Bob & Doug McKenzie	5	14
7/27/85	9/21/85	Take On Me	a-ha	5	22
11/17/79	12/29/79	Take The Long Way Home	Supertramp	10	14
4/9/83	4/30/83	Take The Short Way Home	Dionne Warwick	31	6
7/12/80	8/30/80	Take Your Time (Do It Right) Part 1	S.O.S. Band	8	17
7/19/86	8/30/86	Taken In	Mike + the Mechanics	38	10
6/16/84	7/14/84	Taking It All Too Hard	Genesis	34	8
3/21/87	5/16/87	Talk Dirty To Me	Poison	7	13
1/17/87	2/14/87	Talk To Me	Chico DeBarge	21	7
11/16/85	1/11/86	Talk To Me	Stevie Nicks	15	17
12/17/83	1/28/84	Talking In Your Sleep	Romantics	4	17
5/14/88	6/18/88	Tall Cool One	Robert Plant	12	7
1/25/86	3/8/86	Tarzan Boy	Baltimora	7	13
10/20/84	11/24/84	Teacher Teacher	.38 Special	23	10
11/19/83	12/10/83	Telefone (Long Distance Love Affair)	Sheena Easton	20	9
8/13/83	10/8/83	Tell Her About It	Billy Joel	5	20
12/13/80	1/24/81	Tell It Like It Is	Heart	19	13
1/2/88	1/23/88	Tell It To My Heart	Taylor Dayne	12	10
5/5/84	5/5/84	Tell Me I'm Not Dreamin' (Too Good To Be True)	Jermaine Jackson	46	2
11/19/83	12/10/83	Tender Is The Night	Jackson Browne	27	10
4/12/86	4/26/86	Tender Love	Force M.D.'s	19	7
1/19/85	2/2/85	Tender Years	John Cafferty & the Beaver Brown Band	40	5
3/2/85	3/9/85	Tenderness	General Public	33	6

Debut	Peak	Title	Artist	Pos	Wks
3/13/82	4/10/82	That Girl	Stevie Wonder	9	15
10/11/80	11/15/80	That Girl Could Sing	Jackson Browne	20	12
7/5/86	8/30/86	That Was Then, This Is Now	Monkees	17	13
3/16/85	5/4/85	That Was Yesterday	Foreigner	20	13
12/10/83	1/21/84	That's All	Genesis	13	17
11/15/86	11/22/86	That's Life	David Lee Roth	49	4
12/14/85	2/22/86	That's What Friends Are For	Dionne & Friends	1	19
8/31/85	9/21/85	There Must Be An Angel (Playing With My Heart)	Eurythmics	30	7
4/26/86	7/12/86	There'll Be Sad Songs (To Make You Cry)	Billy Ocean	10	18
4/18/87	5/9/87	There's Nothing Better Than Love	Luther Vandross with Gregory Hines	30	5
1/18/86	3/29/86	These Dreams	Heart	7	17
4/7/84	5/19/84	They Don't Know	Tracy Ullman	10	12
5/11/85	7/13/85	Things Can Only Get Better	Howard Jones	12	16
7/3/82	8/28/82	Think I'm In Love	Eddie Money	15	21
1/14/84	2/11/84	Think Of Laura	Christopher Cross	8	13
4/29/89	5/20/89	Thinking Of You	Sa-Fire	15	6
12/6/80	1/17/81	This Beat Goes On	Kings	9	16
2/8/86	4/5/86	This Could Be The Night	Loverboy	23	12
1/19/80	3/15/80	This Is It	Kenny Loggins	6	23
3/2/85	3/23/85	This Is Not America	David Bowie & the Pat Metheny Group	22	8
6/21/86	7/5/86	This Is The Time	Dennis DeYoung	46	4
12/13/86	1/10/87	This Is The Time	Billy Joel	42	5
5/16/81	6/27/81	This Little Girl	Gary U.S. Bonds	17	14
11/18/89	1/6/90	This One's For The Children	New Kids On The Block	3	14
10/15/83	11/12/83	This Time	Bryan Adams	30	7
1/14/84	3/10/84	Thriller	Michael Jackson	5	21
3/6/82	3/27/82	Through The Years	Kenny Rogers	21	12
8/16/86	10/25/86	Throwing It All Away	Genesis	14	15
12/13/80	2/14/81	Tide Is High, The	Blondie	3	24
11/5/88	11/26/88	Till I Loved You	Barbra Streisand & Don Johnson	15	5
6/27/81	8/1/81	Time	Alan Parsons Project	16	16
5/21/83	6/18/83	Time (Clock Of The Heart)	Culture Club	7	17
5/5/84	6/2/84	Time After Time	Cyndi Lauper	3	17
1/17/81	2/7/81	Time Is Time	Andy Gibb	31	8

Debut	Peak	Title	Artist	Pos	Wks
10/10/87	12/5/87	(I've Had) Time Of My Life, The	Bill Medley & Jennifer Warnes	2	17
4/25/81	5/16/81	Time Out Of Mind	Steely Dan	29	7
12/16/89	1/20/90	Timeless Love	Saraya	14	6
6/14/80	8/2/80	Tired Of Toein' The Line	Rocky Burnette	7	18
3/31/84	5/19/84	To All The Girls I've Loved Before	Julio Iglesias & Willie Nelson	2	23
10/25/86	11/22/86	To Be A Lover	Billy Idol	12	13
11/23/85	1/11/86	To Live And Die In L.A.	Wang Chung	25	12
2/28/81	3/14/81	Together	Tierra	28	8
5/7/88	6/25/88	Together Forever	Rick Astley	3	13
5/23/81	6/27/81	Tom Sawyer	Rush	5	19
4/5/86	5/10/86	Tomorrow Doesn't Matter Tonight	Starship	36	10
4/7/84	5/19/84	Tonight	Kool & the Gang	13	15
11/5/83	12/3/83	Tonight, I Celebrate My Love	Peabo Bryson & Roberta Flack	10	16
7/27/85	10/5/85	Tonight It's You	Cheap Trick	24	15
11/2/85	12/21/85	Tonight She Comes	Cars	10	16
2/14/87	4/4/87	Tonight, Tonight, Tonight	Genesis	3	9
2/16/80	3/29/80	Too Hot	Kool & the Gang	11	16
1/26/85	3/23/85	Too Late For Goodbyes	Julian Lennon	9	17
2/3/90	3/10/90	Too Late To Say Goodbye	Richard Marx	9	7
3/21/81	5/9/81	Too Much Time On My Hands	Styx	4	18
6/18/83	7/23/83	Too Shy	Kajagoogoo	8	14
9/10/83	10/8/83	Total Eclipse Of The Heart	Bonnie Tyler	1	21
1/17/87	2/14/87	Touch Me (I Want Your Body)	Samantha Fox	5	9
7/25/87	9/12/87	Touch Of Grey	Grateful Dead	8	10
5/18/85	6/22/85	Tough All Over	John Cafferty & the Beaver Brown Band	33	9
6/17/89	8/5/89	Toy Soldiers	Martika	1	16
2/2/85	2/23/85	Tragedy	John Hunter	33	8
5/3/80	6/14/80	Train In Vain (Stand By Me)	Clash	15	16
4/20/85	4/20/85	Trapped	Bruce Springsteen	49	1
1/17/81	3/7/81	Treat Me Right	Pat Benatar	10	15
12/12/81	2/6/82	Trouble	Lindsey Buckingham	13	15
10/1/83	10/29/83	True	Spandau Ballet	5	16
10/4/86	11/22/86	True Blue	Madonna	9	15
8/30/86	11/1/86	True Colors	Cyndi Lauper	6	17
12/12/87	1/16/88	True Faith	New Order	13	7

Debut	Peak	Title	Artist	Pos	Wks
8/27/88	9/17/88	True Love	Glenn Frey	23	5
12/27/86	2/7/87	True To You	Ric Ocasek	29	7
11/6/82	12/4/82	Truly	Lionel Richie	1	28
9/12/81	10/24/81	Tryin' To Live My Life Without You	Bob Seger	4	22
5/24/86	7/12/86	Tuff Enuff	Fabulous Thunderbirds	12	12
10/11/80	11/1/80	Turn It On Again	Genesis	31	10
5/23/81	6/13/81	Turn Me Loose	Loverboy	24	12
1/16/82	2/13/82	Turn Your Love Around	George Benson	11	14
9/27/80	11/22/80	Turning Japanese	Vapors	4	21
9/29/79	11/10/79	Tusk	Fleetwood Mac	6	20
10/4/86	10/25/86	25 Or 6 To 4	Chicago	43	4
3/5/83	4/16/83	Twilight Zone	Golden Earring	4	18
7/2/88	7/16/88	Twist (Yo, Twist), The	Fat Boys with Chubby Checker	20	4
12/17/83	1/21/84	Twist Of Fate	Olivia Newton-John	14	15
12/3/88	1/14/89	Two Hearts	Phil Collins	2	12
4/23/88	5/28/88	Two Occasions	Deele	7	7
8/23/86	10/18/86	Two Of Hearts	Stacey Q	1	18
12/27/86	1/10/87	Two People	Tina Turner	55	3
6/21/80	7/5/80	Two Places At The Same Time	Ray Parker, Jr. & Raydio	33	5
12/30/89	2/10/90	Two To Make It Right	Seduction	7	13
8/30/86	10/4/86	Typical Male	Tina Turner	11	14
4/14/90	5/5/90	U Can't Touch This	M.C. Hammer	6	4
7/25/87	10/17/87	U Got The Look	Prince	1	20
11/28/81	1/23/82	Under Pressure	Queen & David Bowie	7	15
11/12/83	12/24/83	Undercover Of The Night	Rolling Stones	7	14
11/3/84	12/8/84	Understanding	Bob Seger & the Silver Bullet Band	20	14
12/3/83	1/14/84	Union Of The Snake	Duran Duran	7	15
9/18/82	10/16/82	Up Where We Belong	Joe Cocker & Jennifer Warnes	1	20
8/9/80	10/4/80	Upside Down	Diana Ross	2	25
10/22/83	12/3/83	Uptown Girl	Billy Joel	4	22
7/4/81	9/26/81	Urgent	Foreigner	2	30
7/24/82	8/21/82	Vacation	Go-Go's	6	14
6/26/82	7/10/82	Valley Girl	Frank Zappa	42	3
12/8/84	1/5/85	Valotte	Julian Lennon	9	13

Debut	Peak	Title	Artist	Pos	Wks
8/2/86	9/6/86	Velcro Fly	ZZ Top	46	7
7/5/86	9/6/86	Venus	Bananarama	1	19
12/27/86	1/24/87	Victory	Kool & the Gang	18	7
5/18/85	7/13/85	View To A Kill, A	Duran Duran	1	17
8/8/81	9/19/81	Voice, The	Moody Blues	11	15
1/26/80	2/23/80	Voices	Cheap Trick	28	9
6/22/85	7/20/85	Voices Carry	'Til Tuesday	15	11
3/23/85	4/27/85	Vox Humana	Kenny Loggins	26	10
3/5/88	5/14/88	Wait	White Lion	1	18
5/9/81	6/20/81	Waiting, The	Tom Petty & the Heartbreakers	12	19
10/10/81	11/21/81	Waiting For A Girl Like You	Foreigner	3	23
12/12/81	1/23/82	Waiting On A Friend	Rolling Stones	13	14
10/13/84	11/10/84	Wake Me Up Before You Go-Go	Wham!	1	18
7/12/86	8/9/86	Walk Like A Man	Mary Jane Girls	23	8
11/1/86	12/13/86	Walk Like An Egyptian	Bangles	1	18
11/2/85	12/21/85	Walk Of Life	Dire Straits	25	16
10/15/88	11/19/88	Walk On Water	Eddie Money	17	7
1/21/89	3/18/89	Walk The Dinosaur	Was (Not Was)	8	12
8/9/86	9/27/86	Walk This Way	Run-D.M.C.	4	15
12/24/88	1/21/89	Walking Away	Information Society	15	6
3/14/87	4/25/87	Walking Down Your Street	Bangles	15	8
10/20/84	11/10/84	Walking On A Thin Line	Huey Lewis & the News	31	10
5/18/85	6/15/85	Walking On Sunshine	Katrina & the Waves	11	13
3/7/81	3/21/81	Walking On Thin Ice	Yoko Ono	23	10
10/11/80	11/29/80	Wanderer, The	Donna Summer	10	17
7/9/83	8/6/83	Wanna Be Startin' Somethin'	Michael Jackson	5	14
4/11/87	5/30/87	Wanted Dead Or Alive	Bon Jovi	10	11
11/19/88	12/31/88	Wap Bam Boogie	Matt Bianco	8	9
11/22/86	12/27/86	War	Bruce Springsteen & the E Street Band	8	8
8/11/84	9/29/84	Warrior, The	Scandal featuring Patty Smyth	11	15
12/30/89	2/10/90	Was It Nothing At All	Michael Damian	4	13
7/24/82	9/4/82	Wasted On The Way	Crosby, Stills & Nash	14	15
3/28/81	5/9/81	Watching The Wheels	John Lennon	13	16
10/11/86	12/13/86	Way It Is, The	Bruce Hornsby & the Range	5	15
9/23/89	11/18/89	(It's Just) Way That You Love Me, The	Paula Abdul	4	16

Debut	Peak	Title	Artist	Pos	Wks
12/10/88	12/31/88	Way You Love Me, The	Karyn White	13	5
11/21/87	1/16/88	Way You Make Me Feel, The	Michael Jackson	3	15
3/23/85	3/30/85	We Are The World	USA For Africa	1	18
11/3/84	12/15/84	We Are The Young	Dan Hartman	17	12
10/27/84	12/22/84	We Belong	Pat Benatar	9	18
9/14/85	11/30/85	We Built This City	Starship	3	22
1/6/90	2/3/90	We Can't Go Wrong	Cover Girls	10	14
2/28/87	3/28/87	We Connect	Stacey Q	19	6
11/11/89	1/6/90	We Didn't Start The Fire	Billy Joel	1	19
6/21/86	8/9/86	We Don't Have To Take Our Clothes Off	Jermaine Stewart	4	15
7/6/85	8/31/85	We Don't Need Another Hero (Thunderdome)	Tina Turner	3	17
12/8/79	2/9/80	We Don't Talk Anymore	Cliff Richard	4	17
2/27/82	4/3/82	We Got The Beat	Go-Go's	2	21
1/2/88	1/30/88	We Said Hello, Goodbye	Phil Collins	22	6
4/11/87	6/6/87	Weatherman Says	Jack Wagner	17	12
3/19/83	5/7/83	Welcome To Heartlight	Kenny Loggins	18	15
10/11/86	11/15/86	Welcome To The Boomtown	David & David	20	12
10/29/88	12/31/88	Welcome To The Jungle	Guns N' Roses	2	16
10/10/87	11/28/87	We'll Be Together	Sting	10	11
10/24/81	11/21/81	We're In This Love Together	Al Jarreau	12	10
8/25/84	9/22/84	We're Not Gonna Take It	Twisted Sister	6	13
12/13/86	2/14/87	We're Ready	Boston	16	11
3/8/86	5/17/86	West End Girls	Pet Shop Boys	1	18
2/19/83	3/26/83	We've Got Tonight	Kenny Rogers & Sheena Easton	10	19
7/20/85	8/31/85	What About Love	Heart	16	14
11/15/86	12/13/86	What About Love	'Til Tuesday	36	5
1/29/83	2/26/83	What About Me	Moving Pictures	11	17
11/10/84	12/1/84	What About Me	Kenny Rogers with Kim Carnes & James Ingram	14	10
12/26/87	2/20/88	What Have I Done To Deserve This	Pet Shop Boys & Dusty Springfield	4	15
4/19/86	5/17/86	What Have You Done For Me Lately	Janet Jackson	7	14
1/21/89	2/25/89	What I Am	Edie Brickell & New Bohemians	2	9
8/5/89	8/26/89	What I Like About You	Michael Morales	22	4
4/21/90	5/5/90	What It Takes	Aerosmith	25	3
6/19/82	7/31/82	What Kind Of Fool Am I	Rick Springfield	21	16

Debut	Peak	Title	Artist	Pos	Wks
1/6/90	2/10/90	What Kind Of Man Would I Be	Chicago	15	10
6/10/89	7/1/89	What You Don't Know	Expose	17	5
2/7/87	3/28/87	What You Get Is What You See	Tina Turner	15	9
2/1/86	4/5/86	What You Need	INXS	7	17
9/17/88	10/1/88	What You See Is What You Get	Brenda K. Starr	22	4
3/21/87	4/25/87	What's Going On	Cyndi Lauper	19	8
7/14/84	9/8/84	What's Love Got To Do With It	Tina Turner	1	22
9/3/88	10/22/88	What's On Your Mind (Pure Energy)	Information Society	8	11
1/30/82	3/13/82	When All Is Said And Done	ABBA	16	11
6/16/84	7/7/84	When Doves Cry	Prince	1	21
10/7/89	11/18/89	When I See You Smile	Bad English	1	19
8/16/86	10/18/86	When I Think Of You	Janet Jackson	3	18
2/16/80	3/8/80	When I Wanted You	Barry Manilow	22	9
12/3/88	2/18/89	When I'm With You	Sheriff	1	17
7/30/88	9/10/88	When It's Love	Van Halen	7	10
4/17/82	6/12/82	When It's Over	Loverboy	21	17
10/10/81	11/14/81	When She Was My Girl	Four Tops	13	14
7/4/87	8/29/87	When Smokey Sings	ABC	19	11
12/10/88	2/4/89	When The Children Cry	White Lion	5	11
12/14/85	2/8/86	When The Going Gets Tough, The Tough Get Going	Billy Ocean	3	19
6/7/86	7/19/86	When The Heart Rules The Mind	GTR	18	12
12/2/89	1/20/90	When The Night Comes	Joe Cocker	4	9
8/6/88	8/20/88	When 2 R In Love	Prince	22	4
8/11/84	9/22/84	When You Close Your Eyes	Night Ranger	9	13
8/10/85	9/21/85	When Your Heart Is Weak	Cock Robin	41	9
5/6/89	6/24/89	Where Are You Now	Jimmy Harnen with Synch	7	10
4/2/88	4/30/88	Where Do Broken Hearts Go	Whitney Houston	5	9
4/5/86	5/17/86	Where Do The Children Go	Hooters	39	7
10/10/87	11/14/87	Where The Streets Have No Name	U2	10	8
3/7/81	4/18/81	While You See A Chance	Steve Winwood	6	18
4/21/90	5/5/90	Whip Appeal	Babyface	18	3
11/8/80	12/20/80	Whip It	Devo	2	36
5/12/84	6/2/84	White Horse	Laid Back	13	11

Debut	Peak	Title	Artist	Pos	Wks
1/7/84	2/11/84	White Lines (Don't Don't Do It)	Grandmaster Flash & Melle Mel	31	15
7/2/83	7/30/83	White Wedding	Billy Idol	8	14
8/14/82	10/30/82	Who Can It Be Now	Men At Work	2	27
5/20/89	6/17/89	Who Do You Give Your Love To	Michael Morales	22	8
9/22/84	10/20/84	Who Wears These Shoes	Elton John	29	10
4/14/90	5/5/90	Whole Wide World	A'me Lorain	15	4
7/18/81	9/19/81	Who's Crying Now	Journey	5	29
7/6/85	8/31/85	Who's Holding Donna Now	DeBarge	8	15
5/10/86	6/28/86	Who's Johnny	El DeBarge	6	15
6/16/84	7/7/84	Who's That Girl	Eurythmics	29	7
7/11/87	8/29/87	Who's That Girl	Madonna	1	20
10/12/85	11/30/85	Who's Zoomin' Who	Aretha Franklin	8	17
3/22/86	4/19/86	Why Can't This Be Love	Van Halen	4	14
12/26/81	1/16/82	Why Do Fools Fall In Love	Diana Ross	19	11
12/10/83	1/14/84	Why Me	Irene Cara	22	13
12/15/79	2/2/80	Why Me	Styx	21	16
7/4/87	7/25/87	Why You Treat Me So Bad	Club Nouveau	27	5
11/3/84	12/8/84	Wild Boys, The	Duran Duran	4	17
2/7/87	3/7/87	Wild Thing	Sister Carol	29	5
12/17/88	1/28/89	Wild Thing	Tone Loc	1	16
8/23/86	10/11/86	Wild Wild Life	Talking Heads	20	16
9/17/88	11/26/88	Wild, Wild West	Escape Club	4	16
6/18/88	7/2/88	Wild, Wild West	Kool Moe Dee	17	5
11/5/88	12/10/88	Wild World	Maxi Priest	15	7
12/20/86	2/21/87	Will You Still Love Me	Chicago	7	12
5/13/89	6/10/89	Wind Beneath My Wings	Bette Midler	1	15
4/16/83	5/7/83	Wind Him Up	Saga	30	8
2/14/81	3/21/81	Winner Takes It All, The	ABBA	12	14
5/30/81	8/1/81	Winning	Santana	3	21
8/29/87	9/26/87	Wipeout	Fat Boys & the Beach Boys	8	12
4/9/88	5/7/88	Wishing Well	Terence Trent D'Arby	3	13
11/18/89	12/16/89	With Every Beat Of My Heart	Taylor Dayne	7	10
3/28/87	5/23/87	With Or Without You	U2	1	16
2/2/80	4/12/80	With You I'm Born Again	Billy Preston & Syreeta	7	23
3/3/90	4/21/90	Without You	Motley Crue	8	10
4/10/82	6/12/82	Without You (Not Another Lonely Night)	Franke & the Knockouts	18	20
1/17/81	3/7/81	Without Your Love	Roger Daltrey	37	15

Debut	Peak	Title	Artist	Pos	Wks
2/14/81	3/21/81	Woman	John Lennon	3	19
9/13/80	10/18/80	Woman In Love	Barbra Streisand	2	23
5/30/81	6/27/81	Woman Needs Love (Just Like You Do), A	Ray Parker, Jr. & Raydio	12	14
10/4/86	11/15/86	Word Up	Cameo	3	17
8/9/86	10/11/86	Words Get In The Way	Miami Sound Machine	4	16
8/14/82	10/9/82	Workin' For A Livin'	Huey Lewis & the News	34	11
1/16/82	2/20/82	Working For The Weekend	Loverboy	9	19
10/3/81	10/24/81	Working In The Coal Mine	Devo	13	12
3/8/80	4/19/80	Working My Way Back To You/Forgive Me, Girl	Spinners	3	19
5/30/87	7/18/87	Wot's It To Ya	Robbie Nevil	28	8
5/25/85	7/13/85	Would I Lie To You	Eurythmics	13	14
11/2/85	12/14/85	Wrap Her Up	Elton John	22	11
1/14/84	2/18/84	Wrapped Around Your Finger	Police	18	15
9/20/80	10/25/80	Xanadu	Olivia Newton-John & Electric Light Orchestra	10	13
12/24/83	2/18/84	Yah Mo B There	James Ingram with Michael McDonald	19	16
8/2/86	8/23/86	Yankee Rose	David Lee Roth	15	10
1/19/80	3/8/80	Yes, I'm Ready	Teri DeSario with KC	5	16
12/5/81	12/26/81	Yesterday's Songs	Neil Diamond	20	10
1/15/83	2/12/83	You And I	Eddie Rabbitt with Crystal Gayle	11	21
2/19/83	4/9/83	You Are	Lionel Richie	5	19
10/19/85	11/30/85	You Are My Lady	Freddie Jackson	6	17
12/13/86	1/24/87	You Be Illin'	Run-D.M.C.	13	8
9/14/85	11/23/85	You Belong To The City	Glenn Frey	1	19
3/21/81	5/2/81	You Better You Bet	Who	2	18
8/9/86	10/4/86	You Can Call Me Al	Paul Simon	28	15
4/4/87	5/30/87	You Can Call Me Al	Paul Simon	8	13
9/11/82	10/30/82	You Can Do Magic	America	6	19
6/2/84	6/30/84	You Can't Get What You Want (Till You Know What You Want)	Joe Jackson	18	10
12/11/82	1/8/83	You Can't Hurry Love	Phil Collins	12	16
10/20/79	11/17/79	You Decorated My Life	Kenny Rogers	14	16
7/6/85	8/10/85	You Give Good Love	Whitney Houston	7	19
10/11/86	11/29/86	You Give Love A Bad Name	Bon Jovi	1	16

Debut	Peak	Title	Artist	Pos	Wks
12/17/88	2/11/89	You Got It (The Right Stuff)	New Kids On The Block	11	12
2/7/87	3/14/87	You Got It All	Jets	10	8
11/27/82	1/8/83	You Got Lucky	Tom Petty & the Heartbreakers	20	15
4/11/87	6/13/87	You Keep Me Hangin' On	Kim Wilde	2	16
9/25/82	10/16/82	You Keep Runnin' Away	.38 Special	27	8
10/18/86	12/6/86	You Know I Love You...Don't You	Howard Jones	28	13
7/18/81	8/8/81	You Make My Dreams	Daryl Hall & John Oates	24	11
3/22/80	5/17/80	You May Be Right	Billy Joel	10	28
3/24/84	5/5/84	You Might Think	Cars	8	18
11/15/80	1/10/81	You Shook Me All Night Long	AC/DC	15	26
7/5/86	8/16/86	You Should Be Mine (The Woo Woo Song)	Jeffrey Osborne	24	11
8/7/82	10/2/82	You Should Hear How She Talks About You	Melissa Manchester	3	18
7/6/85	8/24/85	You Spin Me Round (Like A Record)	Dead Or Alive	14	13
9/28/85	11/9/85	You Wear It Well	El DeBarge with DeBarge	37	8
8/30/80	10/4/80	You'll Accomp'ny Me	Bob Seger	14	13
4/4/87	4/25/87	Young Blood	Bruce Willis	31	5
11/21/81	1/16/82	Young Turks	Rod Stewart	3	19
3/15/86	5/24/86	Your Love	Outfield	6	16
1/8/83	1/29/83	Your Love Is Driving Me Crazy	Sammy Hagar	23	13
2/18/89	4/8/89	Your Mama Don't Dance	Poison	6	10
4/26/86	6/21/86	Your Wildest Dreams	Moody Blues	16	17
11/16/85	1/25/86	You're A Friend Of Mine	Clarence Clemons & Jackson Browne	11	16
2/18/89	3/18/89	You're Not Alone	Chicago	20	6
7/20/85	9/21/85	You're Only Human (Second Wind)	Billy Joel	15	15
12/1/79	12/29/79	You're Only Lonely	J.D. Souther	12	14
11/24/84	2/2/85	You're The Inspiration	Chicago	6	18
9/6/80	10/11/80	You're The Only Woman (You & I)	Ambrosia	23	10
5/13/89	6/24/89	Youth Gone Wild	Skid Row	14	10
10/16/82	11/20/82	You've Got Another Thing Comin'	Judas Priest	20	13
11/22/80	12/20/80	You've Lost That Lovin' Feeling	Daryl Hall & John Oates	19	15

YEARLY TOP 40 CHARTS

Top Hits of 1980:

1.	Another One Bites The Dust	Queen
2.	Call Me	Blondie
3.	(Just Like) Starting Over	John Lennon
4.	Magic	Olivia Newton-John
5.	It's Still Rock & Roll To Me	Billy Joel
6.	Comin' Up (Live At Glasgow)	
		Paul McCartney & Wings
7.	Rock With You	Michael Jackson
8.	Escape (The Pina Colada Song)	Rupert Holmes
9.	Lost In Love	Air Supply
10.	Another Brick In The Wall	Pink Floyd
11.	Lady	Kenny Rogers
12.	Crazy Little Thing Called Love	Queen
13.	Woman In Love	Barbra Streisand
14.	Whip It	Devo
15.	Sailing	Christopher Cross
16.	Upside Down	Diana Ross
17.	The Rose	Bette Midler
18.	Coward Of The County	Kenny Rogers
19.	Ride Like The Wind	Christopher Cross
20.	Please Don't Go	KC & the Sunshine Band
21.	All Out Of Love	Air Supply
22.	Funkytown	Lipps, Inc.
23.	Emotional Rescue	Rolling Stones

24.	Working My Way Back To You/Forgive Me, Girl	
		Spinners
25.	Gimme Some Lovin'	Blues Brothers
26.	I'm Alright	Kenny Loggins
27.	Longer	Dan Fogelberg
28.	Brass In Pocket (I'm Special)	Pretenders
29.	Turning Japanese	Vapors
30.	Steal Away	Robbie Dupree
31.	We Don't Talk Anymore	Cliff Richard
32.	Misunderstanding	Genesis
33.	Against The Wind	Bob Seger
34.	Hungry Heart	Bruce Springsteen
35.	Do That To Me One More Time	Captain & Tennille
36.	Drivin' My Life Away	Eddie Rabbitt
37.	Cars	Gary Numan
38.	Games Without Frontiers	Peter Gabriel
39.	Jesse	Carly Simon
40.	On The Radio	Donna Summer

Top Hits of 1981:

1.	Endless Love	Diana Ross & Lionel Richie
2.	9 To 5	Dolly Parton
3.	Bette Davis Eyes	Kim Carnes
4.	Physical	Olivia Newton-John
5.	Jessie's Girl	Rick Springfield
6.	Keep On Loving You	REO Speedwagon
7.	Private Eyes	Daryl Hall & John Oates
8.	Morning Train (9 To 5)	Sheena Easton
9.	The Stroke	Billy Squier
10.	Start Me Up	Rolling Stones
11.	Celebration	Kool & the Gang
12.	Stars On 45	Stars On 45
13.	You Better, You Bet	Who
14.	Hit Me With Your Best Shot	Pat Benatar
15.	Urgent	Foreigner
16.	Theme From "Greatest American Hero"	Joey Scarbury
17.	Rapture	Blondie
18.	Waiting For A Girl Like You	Foreigner
19.	Arthur's Theme (Best That You Can Do)	
		Christopher Cross
20.	Woman	John Lennon
21.	I Love You	Climax Blues Band
22.	Kiss On My List	Daryl Hall & John Oates
23.	All Those Years Ago	George Harrison
24.	The Tide Is High	Blondie
25.	Winning	Santana
26.	Tryin' To Live My Life Without You	Bob Seger
27.	The Best Of Times	Styx
28.	Too Much Time On My Hands	Styx

29.	Queen Of Hearts	Juice Newton
30.	I Love A Rainy Night	Eddie Rabbitt
31.	In The Air Tonight	Phil Collins
32.	The Night Owls	Little River Band
33.	Who's Crying Now	Journey
34.	Angel Of The Morning	Juice Newton
35.	Hold On Loosely	.38 Special
36.	Take It On The Run	REO Speedwagon
37.	Tom Sawyer	Rush
38.	The One That You Love	Air Supply
39.	For Your Eyes Only	Sheena Easton
40.	Every Little Thing She Does Is Magic	Police

Top Hits of 1982:

1.	I Love Rock 'N Roll	Joan Jett & the Blackhearts
2.	Centerfold	J. Geils Band
3.	Eye Of The Tiger	Survivor
4.	Mickey	Toni Basil
5.	Up Where We Belong	Joe Cocker & Jennifer Warnes
6.	Hard To Say I'm Sorry/Getaway	Chicago
7.	Ebony & Ivory	Paul McCartney with Stevie Wonder
8.	Jack & Diane	John Cougar
9.	Chariots Of Fire - Titles	Vangelis
10.	Truly	Lionel Richie
11.	Gloria	Laura Branigan
12.	Don't You Want Me	Human League
13.	Our Lips Are Sealed	Go-Go's
14.	We Got The Beat	Go-Go's
15.	Who Can It Be Now	Men At Work
16.	Hurts So Good	John Cougar
17.	Abracadabra	Steve Miller Band
18.	I Can't Go For That (No Can Do)	
		Daryl Hall & John Oates
19.	Steppin' Out	Joe Jackson
20.	'65 Love Affair	Paul Davis
21.	Rosanna	Toto
22.	Harden My Heart	Quarterflash
23.	Freeze-Frame	J. Geils Band
24.	You Should Hear How She Talks About You	
		Melissa Manchester
25.	The Other Woman	Ray Parker, Jr.
26.	Eye In The Sky	Alan Parsons Project
27.	Dirty Laundry	Don Henley

28.	Young Turks	Rod Stewart
29.	Pac-Man Fever	Buckner & Garcia
30.	Open Arms	Journey
31.	Rock This Town	Stray Cats
32.	Key Largo	Bertie Higgins
33.	Heart Attack	Olivia Newton-John
34.	867-5309/Jenny	Tommy Tutone
35.	Hold Me	Fleetwood Mac
36.	I Ran (So Far Away)	Flock Of Seagulls
37.	Don't Fight It	Kenny Loggins with Steve Perry
38.	Love Is Like A Rock	Donnie Iris
39.	Take Off	Bob & Doug McKenzie
40.	Somebody's Baby	Jackson Browne

Top Hits of 1983:

1.	Flashdance… What A Feeling	Irene Cara
2.	Billie Jean	Michael Jackson
3.	Baby, Come To Me	Patti Austin with James Ingram
4.	The Curly Shuffle	Jump 'n the Saddle
5.	Total Eclipse Of The Heart	Bonnie Tyler
6.	Every Breath You Take	Police
7.	Electric Avenue	Eddy Grant
8.	Beat It	Michael Jackson
9.	All Night Long (All Night)	Lionel Richie
10.	Sweet Dreams (Are Made Of This)	Eurythmics
11.	Mr. Roboto	Styx
12.	Islands In The Stream	Kenny Rogers with Dolly Parton
13.	The Safety Dance	Men Without Hats
14.	Say Say Say	Paul McCartney & Michael Jackson
15.	Down Under	Men At Work
16.	Maneater	Daryl Hall & John Oates
17.	Let's Dance	David Bowie
18.	Hungry Like The Wolf	Duran Duran
19.	Puttin' On The Ritz	Taco
20.	Shame On The Moon	Bob Seger & the Silver Bullet Band
21.	Never Gonna Let You Go	Sergio Mendes
22.	Making Love Out Of Nothing At All	Air Supply
23.	She Works Hard For The Money	Donna Summer
24.	Come On Eileen	Dexys Midnight Runners
25.	Cum On Feel The Noize	Quiet Riot
26.	Africa	Toto
27.	Do You Really Want To Hurt Me	Culture Club
28.	She Blinded Me With Science	Thomas Dolby

29.	Little Red Corvette	Prince
30.	Maniac	Michael Sembello
31.	Jeopardy	Greg Kihn Band
32.	Twilight Zone	Golden Earring
33.	Uptown Girl	Billy Joel
34.	Stray Cat Strut	Stray Cats
35.	Ewok Celebration	Meco
36.	Always Something There To Remind Me	Naked Eyes
37.	True	Spandau Ballet
38.	Wanna Be Startin' Somethin'	Michael Jackson
39.	Tell Her About It	Billy Joel
40.	You Are	Lionel Richie

Top Hits of 1984:

1.	Ghostbusters	Ray Parker, Jr.
2.	I Just Called To Say I Love You	Stevie Wonder
3.	Footloose	Kenny Loggins
4.	What's Love Got To Do With It	Tina Turner
5.	Hello	Lionel Richie
6.	When Doves Cry	Prince
7.	Wake Me Up Before You Go-Go	Wham!
8.	99 Red Balloons/99 Luftballons	Nena
9.	Karma Chameleon	Culture Club
10.	The Reflex	Duran Duran
11.	I Feel For You	Chaka Khan
12.	Cool It Now	New Edition
13.	Let's Hear It For The Boy	Deniece Williams
14.	Somebody's Watching Me	Rockwell
15.	Break My Stride	Matthew Wilder
16.	Against All Odds (Take A Look At Me Now)	
		Phil Collins
17.	She Bop	Cyndi Lauper
18.	I'm So Excited	Pointer Sisters
19.	Jump	Van Halen
20.	To All The Girls I've Loved Before	
		Julio Iglesias & Willie Nelson
21.	Purple Rain	Prince & the Revolution
22.	Sister Christian	Night Ranger
23.	Let's Go Crazy	Prince & the Revolution
24.	Dancing In The Dark	Bruce Springsteen
25.	I Guess That's Why They Call It The Blues	
		Elton John
26.	Eat It	"Weird Al" Yankovic

27.	Missing You	John Waite
28.	Caribbean Queen (No More Love On The Run)	
		Billy Ocean
29.	Strut	Sheena Easton
30.	Time After Time	Cyndi Lauper
31.	Girls Just Want To Have Fun	Cyndi Lauper
32.	Sea Of Love	Honeydrippers
33.	The Glamorous Life	Sheila E.
34.	Talking In Your Sleep	Romantics
35.	Borderline	Madonna
36.	Owner Of A Lonely Heart	Yes
37.	The Wild Boys	Duran Duran
38.	Self Control	Laura Branigan
39.	Joanna	Kool & the Gang
40.	Hold Me Now	Thompson Twins

Top Hits of 1985:

1.	We Are The World	USA For Africa
2.	Money For Nothing	Dire Straits
3.	Separate Lives	Phil Collins & Marilyn Martin
4.	Axel F	Harold Faltermeyer
5.	Miami Vice Theme	Jan Hammer
6.	Careless Whisper	Wham!
7.	Shout	Tears For Fears
8.	The Heat Is On	Glenn Frey
9.	Say You, Say Me	Lionel Richie
10.	Everybody Wants To Rule The World	
		Tears For Fears
11.	Like A Virgin	Madonna
12.	Easy Lover	Philip Bailey with Phil Collins
13.	A View To A Kill	Duran Duran
14.	Oh Sheila	Ready For The World
15.	Do They Know It's Christmas	Band Aid
16.	Cherish	Kool & the Gang
17.	St. Elmo's Fire (Man In Motion)	John Parr
18.	You Belong To The City	Glenn Frey
19.	Crazy For You	Madonna
20.	The Power Of Love	Huey Lewis & the News
21.	Material Girl	Madonna
22.	Don't You (Forget About Me)	Simple Minds
23.	Sussudio	Phil Collins
24.	Saving All My Love For You	Whitney Houston
25.	I Want To Know What Love Is	Foreigner
26.	Party All The Time	Eddie Murphy
27.	We Don't Need Another Hero	Tina Turner
28.	Rhythm Of The Night	DeBarge

29.	All I Need	Jack Wagner
30.	One More Night	Phil Collins
31.	We Built This City	Starship
32.	Broken Wings	Mr. Mister
33.	Can't Fight This Feeling	REO Speedwagon
34.	Never Surrender	Corey Hart
35.	Into The Groove	Madonna
36.	I Miss You	Klymaxx
37.	Dancing In The Street	Mick Jagger & David Bowie
38.	Loverboy	Billy Ocean
39.	Heaven	Bryan Adams
40.	Part-Time Lover	Stevie Wonder

Top Hits of 1986:

1.	On My Own	Patti LaBelle & Michael McDonald
2.	Walk Like An Egyptian	Bangles
3.	Papa Don't Preach	Madonna
4.	Superbowl Shuffle	Chicago Bears Shufflin' Crew
5.	How Will I Know	Whitney Houston
6.	Friends & Lovers	Gloria Loring & Carl Anderson
7.	Kiss	Prince & the Revolution
8.	Two Of Hearts	Stacey Q
9.	Rock Me Amadeus	Falco
10.	Amanda	Boston
11.	Venus	Bananarama
12.	You Give Love A Bad Name	Bon Jovi
13.	That's What Friends Are For	Dionne & Friends
14.	Addicted To Love	Robert Palmer
15.	West End Girls	Pet Shop Boys
16.	Greatest Love Of All	Whitney Houston
17.	Holding Back The Years	Simply Red
18.	Glory Of Love	Peter Cetera
19.	Human	Human League
20.	Live To Tell	Madonna
21.	Sledgehammer	Peter Gabriel
22.	Stand By Me	Ben E. King
23.	Crush On You	Jets
24.	Kyrie	Mr. Mister
25.	Stuck With You	Huey Lewis & the News
26.	When I Think Of You	Janet Jackson
27.	When The Going Gets Tough, The Tough Get Going	Billy Ocean
28.	Word Up	Cameo

29.	Nasty	Janet Jackson
30.	Secret Lovers	Atlantic Starr
31.	I Didn't Mean To Turn You On	Robert Palmer
32.	Conga	Miami Sound Machine
33.	Everybody Have Fun Tonight	Wang Chung
34.	Dancing On The Ceiling	Lionel Richie
35.	Walk This Way	Run-D.M.C.
36.	I Can't Wait	Nu Shooz
37.	Why Can't This Be Love	Van Halen
38.	Mad About You	Belinda Carlisle
39.	Rumors	Timex Social Club
40.	I Wanna Be A Cowboy	Boys Don't Cry

Top Hits of 1987:

1.	I Want Your Sex	George Michael
2.	Here I Go Again	Whitesnake
3.	Livin' On A Prayer	Bon Jovi
4.	Heaven Is A Place On Earth	Belinda Carlisle
5.	I Think We're Alone Now	Tiffany
6.	I Wanna Dance With Somebody (Who Loves Me)	
		Whitney Houston
7.	Lean On Me	Club Nouveau
8.	Always	Atlantic Starr
9.	La Bamba	Los Lobos
10.	Alone	Prince
11.	U Got The Look	Daryl Hall & John Oates
12.	Keep Your Hands To Yourself	Georgia Satellites
13.	Looking For A New Love	Jody Watley
14.	Faith	George Michael
15.	With Or Without You	U2
16.	Nothing's Gonna Stop Us Now	Starship
17.	At This Moment	Billy Vera & the Beaters
18.	Mony Mony "Live"	Billy Idol
19.	Don't Dream It's Over	Crowded House
20.	Who's That Girl	Madonna
21.	(I Just) Died In Your Arms	Cutting Crew
22.	Luka	Suzanne Vega
23.	Didn't We Almost Have It All	Whitney Houston
24.	Head To Toe	Lisa Lisa & Cult Jam
25.	Songbird	Kenny G
26.	(You Gotta) Fight For Your Right (To Party)	
		Beastie Boys
27.	Come Go With Me	Expose

28.	The Lady In Red	Chris DeBurgh
29.	Shakedown	Bob Seger
30.	(I've Had) The Time Of My Life	
		Bill Medley & Jennifer Warnes
31.	You Keep Me Hangin' On	Kim Wilde
32.	Notorious	Duran Duran
33.	Love You Down	Ready For The World
34.	Somewhere Out There	
		Linda Ronstadt & James Ingram
35.	Only In My Dreams	Debbie Gibson
36.	Funky Town	Pseudo Echo
37.	C'est La Vie	Robbie Nevil
38.	La Isla Bonita	Madonna
39.	I Still Haven't Found What I'm Looking For	U2
40.	I Just Can't Stop Loving You	Michael Jackson

Top Hits of 1988:

1.	Kokomo	Beach Boys
2.	Pump Up The Volume	M/A/R/R/S
3.	Every Rose Has Its Thorn	Poison
4.	Could've Been	Tiffany
5.	Got My Mind Set On You	George Harrison
6.	Wait	White Lion
7.	Dirty Diana	Michael Jackson
8.	Pink Cadillac	Natalie Cole
9.	One More Try	George Michael
10.	Get Outta My Dreams, Get Into My Car	Billy Ocean
11.	Roll With It	Steve Winwood
12.	Red Red Wine	UB40
13.	Don't Worry Be Happy	Bobby McFerrin
14.	The Flame	Cheap Trick
15.	Hands To Heaven	Breathe
16.	Pour Some Sugar On Me	Def Leppard
17.	Never Gonna Give You Up	Rick Astley
18.	Endless Summer Nights	Richard Marx
19.	Shattered Dreams	Johnny Hates Jazz
20.	Groovy Kind Of Love	Phil Collins
21.	Sweet Child O' Mine	Guns N' Roses
22.	Love Bites	Def Leppard
23.	Monkey	George Michael
24.	Simply Irresistible	Robert Palmer
25.	Man In The Mirror	Michael Jackson
26.	Welcome To The Jungle	Guns N' Roses
27.	Hazy Shade Of Winter	Bangles
28.	Naughty Girls (Need Love Too)	Samantha Fox
29.	Hungry Eyes	Eric Carmen

30.	Desire	U2
31.	Father Figure	George Michael
32.	Out Of The Blue	Debbie Gibson
33.	Look Away	Chicago
34.	Mercedes Boy	Pebbles
35.	Push It	Salt-N-Pepa
36.	Foolish Beat	Debbie Gibson
37.	A Nightmare On My Street	
		D.J. Jazzy Jeff & the Fresh Prince
38.	Fast Car	Tracy Chapman
39.	Wishing Well	Terence Trent D'Arby
40.	Kiss Me Deadly	Lita Ford

Top Hits of 1989:

1.	Pump Up The Jam	Technotronic featuring Felly
2.	Like A Prayer	Madonna
3.	Girl I'm Gonna Miss You	Milli Vanilli
4.	When I See You Smile	Bad English
5.	Straight Up	Paula Abdul
6.	Right Here Waiting	Richard Marx
7.	Baby Don't Forget My Number	Milli Vanilli
8.	Wild Thing	Tone Loc
9.	Patience	Guns N' Roses
10.	Eternal Flame	Bangles
11.	Toy Soldiers	Martika
12.	Miss You Much	Janet Jackson
13.	The Living Years	Mike + the Mechanics
14.	Once Bitten Twice Shy	Great White
15.	Rock On	Michael Damian
16.	When I'm With You	Sheriff
17.	Buffalo Stance	Neneh Cherry
18.	Wind Beneath My Wings	Bette Midler
19.	Lost In Your Eyes	Debbie Gibson
20.	Bust A Move	Young MC
21.	Hangin' Tough/Didn't I (Blow Your Mind)	New Kids On The Block
22.	Girl You Know It's True	Milli Vanilli
23.	If I Could Turn Back Time	Cher
24.	Swing The Mood	Jive Bunny & the Mastermixers
25.	Heaven	Warrant
26.	Blame It On The Rain	Milli Vanilli
27.	Cult Of Personality	Living Colour
28.	Good Thing	Fine Young Cannibals

29.	Another Day In Paradise	Phil Collins
30.	Funky Cold Medina	Tone Loc
31.	She Wants To Dance With Me	Rick Astley
32.	Cover Girl	New Kids On The Block
33.	Love Song	Cure
34.	If You Don't Know Me By Now	Simply Red
35.	Two Hearts	Phil Collins
36.	I Wanna Have Some Fun	Samantha Fox
37.	Dr. Feelgood	Motley Crue
38.	What I Am	Edie Brickell & New Bohemians
39.	Cold Hearted	Paula Abdul
40.	Angelia	Richard Marx

Top Hits of 1990:

The WYTZ Street Sheet ceased publication after the May 5, 1990 survey, concluding nearly thirty straight years of charts published by WLS-AM and its FM "sister station". Here are the top ten tunes of the first four months of 1990.

1.	We Didn't Start The Fire	Billy Joel
2.	Opposites Attract	Paula Abdul
3.	Black Velvet	Alannah Myles
4.	How Am I Supposed To Live Without You	
		Michael Bolton
5.	Escapade	Janet Jackson
6.	Nothing Compares 2 U	Sinead O'Connor
7.	Get Up (Before The Night Is Over)	Technotronic
8.	Free Fallin'	Tom Petty
9.	I Remember You	Skid Row
10.	Dangerous	Roxette

TOP 40 SONGS OF THE 1980s

1.	Another One Bites The Dust	Queen
2.	Endless Love	Diana Ross & Lionel Richie
3.	We Are The World	USA For Africa
4.	I Love Rock 'N Roll	Joan Jett & the Blackhearts
5.	Centerfold	J. Geils Band
6.	Call Me	Blondie
7.	9 To 5	Dolly Parton
8.	Bette Davis Eyes	Kim Carnes
9.	Eye Of The Tiger	Survivor
10.	Mickey	Toni Basil
11.	On My Own	Patti LaBelle & Michael McDonald
12.	Kokomo	Beach Boys
13.	Physical	Olivia Newton-John
14.	Flashdance... What A Feeling	Irene Cara
15.	Billie Jean	Michael Jackson
16.	(Just Like) Starting Over	John Lennon
17.	Up Where We Belong	Joe Cocker & Jennifer Warnes
18.	Baby, Come To Me	Patti Austin with James Ingram
19.	The Curly Shuffle	Jump 'n the Saddle
20.	Walk Like An Egyptian	Bangles
21.	Papa Don't Preach	Madonna
22.	Pump Up The Volume	M/A/R/R/S
23.	Superbowl Shuffle	Chicago Bears Shufflin' Crew
24.	Hard To Say I'm Sorry/Getaway	Chicago
25.	Jessie's Girl	Rick Springfield

156

26.	Magic	Olivia Newton-John
27.	Ghostbusters	Ray Parker, Jr.
28.	Ebony & Ivory	Paul McCartney with Stevie Wonder
29.	Total Eclipse Of The Heart	Bonnie Tyler
30.	I Just Called To Say I Love You	Stevie Wonder
31.	Money For Nothing	Dire Straits
32.	Every Rose Has Its Thorn	Poison
33.	Keep On Loving You	REO Speedwagon
34.	Private Eyes	Daryl Hall & John Oates
35.	Every Breath You Take	Police
36.	Pump Up The Jam	Technotronic featuring Felly
37.	Footloose	Kenny Loggins
38.	It's Still Rock & Roll To Me	Billy Joel
39.	Comin' Up (Live At Glasgow)	Paul McCartney & Wings
40.	Rock With You	Michael Jackson

Big 89 Artists of the 1980s

1. Madonna
2. Prince
3. Michael Jackson
4. Phil Collins
5. Lionel Richie
6. George Michael/Wham!
7. Billy Joel
8. Huey Lewis & the News
9. Daryl Hall & John Oates
10. Journey
11. Bob Seger
12. Genesis
13. John Cougar Mellencamp
14. Duran Duran
15. Kool & the Gang
16. Whitney Houston
17. Kenny Rogers
18. Chicago
19. Kenny Loggins
20. Elton John
21. Def Leppard
22. Stevie Wonder
23. Tom Petty & the Heartbreakers
24. Bon Jovi
25. Bruce Springsteen

26. Gloria Estefan/Miami Sound Machine
27. Pat Benatar
28. Jefferson Starship/Starship
29. Bryan Adams
30. Air Supply
31. Rick Springfield
32. Janet Jackson
33. Pointer Sisters
34. Paul McCartney
35. Heart
36. Billy Ocean
37. Sheena Easton
38. Survivor
39. Cyndi Lauper
40. REO Speedwagon
41. Olivia Newton-John
42. Tina Turner
43. Rolling Stones
44. Police
45. Culture Club
46. Richard Marx
47. Van Halen
48. Poison
49. Diana Ross
50. Bangles
51. Rod Stewart
52. Stevie Nicks
53. Foreigner
54. Debbie Gibson
55. Loverboy
56. Don Henley
57. Cars

58.   Steve Winwood
59.   Joan Jett & the Blackhearts
60.   Eurythmics
61.   Peter Gabriel
62.   Jackson Browne
63.   David Bowie
64.   New Kids On The Block
65.   Jets
66.   INXS
67.   U2
68.   Ray Parker, Jr.
69.   Christopher Cross
70.   .38 Special
71.   Pretenders
72.   Night Ranger
73.   Bobby Brown
74.   Electric Light Orchestra
75.   Glenn Frey
76.   Cheap Trick
77.   Neil Diamond
78.   Queen
79.   Fleetwood Mac
80.   Guns N' Roses
81.   Belinda Carlisle
82.   Corey Hart
83.   Linda Ronstadt
84.   Dionne Warwick
85.   Robert Palmer
86.   Styx
87.   Taylor Dayne
88.   Thompson Twins
89.   Toto

ABOUT THE AUTHOR

Ron Smith is a 30-year veteran of oldies radio as a disk jockey, program and music director. He served for more than eight years as Music Director of WJMK-FM, Oldies 104.3 in Chicago and was Senior Music Programmer of Internet Radio for RadioWave.com in the Windy City. Since 1995, he has delighted fans of 50s, 60s and 70s music with the Internet's premiere oldies Web site—www.oldiesmusic.com.

He is also the author of *Chicago Top 40 Charts 1960-1969* and *Chicago Top 40 Charts 1970-1979*. He resides in suburban Chicago with his vast music and book libraries.

0-595-22626-4

Printed in the United States
5905